Miniature
CROCHET

Projects in 1/12 Scale

Miniature
CROCHET

Projects in 1/12 Scale

Roz Walters

GUILD OF MASTER CRAFTSMAN PUBLICATIONS

First published 2003 by
Guild of Master Craftsman Publications Ltd
Castle Place, 166 High Street,
Lewes, East Sussex BN7 1XU

Reprinted 2005

ISBN 1 86108 273 8

A catalogue record for this book is available from the British Library.

Editor: Stephen Haynes
Designer: Danny McBride
Photographer: Anthony Bailey
Illustrator: Penny Brown

Set in Sabon, Humanist and Cochin

Colour origination by Universal Graphics, Singapore
Printed and bound by Sino Publishing House Ltd. China

CONTENTS

Preface

I have always loved making things, needlework especially. From an early age I made clothes for my family and myself, using my grandmother's old treadle sewing machine. My grandmother taught me to crochet, starting with thick wool before introducing me to the finer crochet and tatting threads. I hope she would be impressed with my use of the even finer bobbin-lacemaking threads used on many of the projects in this book.

Having created several designs for one of the specialist miniaturist magazines, my thoughts turned to a wider readership, in book form. I have tried in this volume to create designs for all, from the complete beginner to the experienced crocheter. Some projects will only take an hour or so to complete, others several days or weeks.

There are over 40 projects in the book; many are interchangeable. A lady may wish to own a V-necked jumper. Why should such a garment be the preserve of men? Even though you may not own a four-poster bed, you may still enjoy creating the blanket, bedspread, sheet and pillow edgings for something less grandiose.

Some miniaturists choose not to have 'people' in their dolls' houses. However, I am sure there would still be clothes hanging in the wardrobe or neatly folded in a drawer. A stole draped over the back of a chair, or a hat thrown carelessly onto the bed, each serve to denote occupancy of your miniature home.

Whatever your skill level, I am sure you will find this book a useful addition to your miniature-making library. I hope you have as much pleasure in recreating some – if not all – of these 1/12 scale projects as I have had in designing them.

HOW TO WORK THE STITCHES

Crochet requires few tools and can be learnt in a matter of minutes; once the basic chain and

double crochet have been mastered, all other stitches are a variation of double crochet.

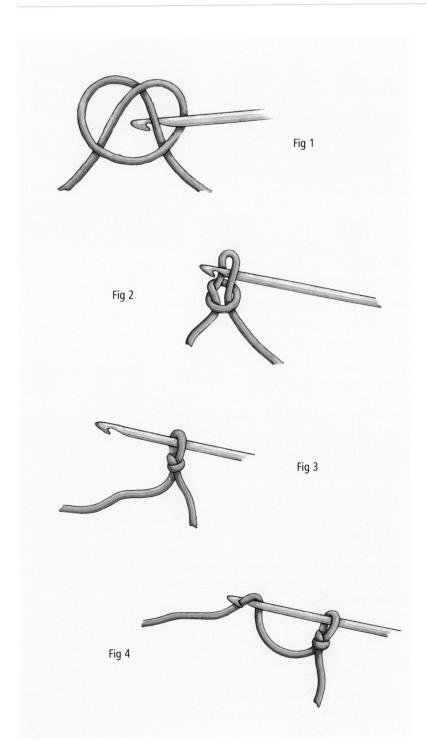

Fig 1

Fig 2

Fig 3

Fig 4

Slipknot

To make a slipknot, hold the hook in your right hand and the yarn in your left. Make a loop, insert the hook into the loop and pull through (Fig 1).

Chain

Make a slipknot on the hook, leaving approximately 10cm (4in) tail (Fig 2).

Pull up to close the loop near the hook, but not too tightly (Fig 3).

Pass the yarn over the hook (Fig 4; the technical term for this is *yarn over*) and pull through the loop.

First chain made, repeat for the number of chains required. Note that when counting the number of chains you do not include the slipknot at the beginning.

The first row of chain stitches made is called the foundation chain, and forms the basis for the double crochet, treble crochet and other stitches.

Double crochet

Work the first double crochet into the second chain from the hook, as follows. Insert hook into second chain. Do not count the chain on the hook as the first chain. Yarn over the hook; there are now two loops on the hook. Pull yarn through both loops, and the first stitch is made. Fig 5 shows the end result.

Repeat to the end of the row. Work one chain at the end of this row (this is known as the turning chain), then turn the work around. The chain usually counts as the first stitch in the new row.

In the next and all subsequent rows, miss the first stitch, then work one double crochet in each of the existing double crochets, making sure one double crochet is worked in the turning chain at the end of each row. If in doubt, it helps to count the stitches as you work: for example, '14 chain' would produce 13 double crochets plus the turning chain. On subsequent rows, miss the first double crochet, then make one double crochet in each of the next 12 double crochets, one double crochet in the turning chain, one chain, turn.

Treble

Yarn over hook; insert hook into the third chain from the hook.

Yarn over hook and draw through the first two loops; yarn over hook and draw through the last two loops. Work one treble in each chain to the end of the row, ending with three chain, turn. As with double crochet, it is usual to miss the first stitch in subsequent rows.

Half treble

Yarn over hook; insert hook into the third chain from the hook; yarn over hook and draw through all the loops. Work as double crochet or treble, ending with two chain, turn.

Double treble

Yarn over the hook twice, insert hook into fifth chain from hook, yarn over hook and draw through the first two loops; yarn over hook and draw through the next two loops; yarn over hook and draw through the last two loops.

Slipstitch

Hook through initial slipknot, then pull through both loops.

This stitch is used for joining, especially on anything worked in the round: hats, tablecloths, parasol, etc. For example, work four chain and join with a slipstitch into a ring, three chain, work seven double crochet into ring, and join with a slipstitch. Work is not turned when working in

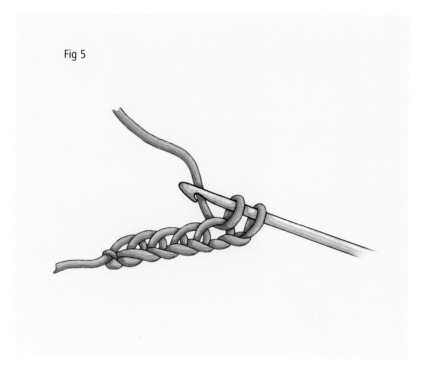

Fig 5

rounds; this gives a very different appearance to the work.

Slipstitches are also used to avoid joining yarn. Instead of cutting the yarn, work a slipstitch in each stitch until the required point is reached. Work the required number of chain for the stitch and carry on as before. This is not recommended for more than two or three stitches. Used at an armhole or near an edge, this method saves breaking the thread and having to sew in the ends.

When joining yarn – to work a sleeve, for instance – use a slipstitch and then work one, two or three chain before working the next double crochet, half treble or treble in the next stitch.

Increasing

Work two stitches into one existing stitch. Some increases are created by working into the normally missed first stitch on a row.

Decreasing (working 2 tog)

Work the first half of the first stitch, leaving the last two loops on the hook. Now work the first

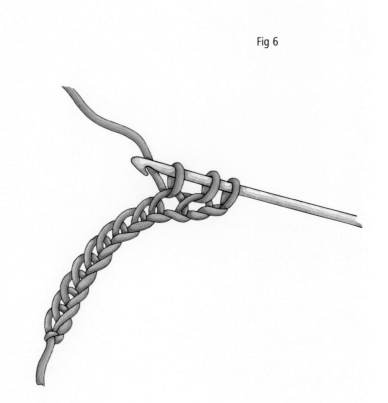

Fig 6

half of the next stitch (which makes a third loop), yarn over, and pull through all three loops at once, thus creating one stitch from two (Fig 6).

Joining yarn mid-row

Work the first half of the stitch with the old yarn, then the second half with the new yarn. This method also works well when you are changing to a new colour.

Right and wrong sides

With the right side facing you, the length of yarn from the foundation chain should be at the left-hand side.

Tension

On such a small scale, tension is not really a problem – a stitch here or there is not really going to make any difference. Like humans, dolls' house people are all different shapes and sizes; try the garments as you go along. If you find there is a large discrepancy in the size, use a smaller or larger hook. To make fitted gathers at the waist or sleeve, thread a length of yarn through, pull up to fit, tie with a reef knot and sew in the ends.

ABBREVIATIONS

The following abbreviations are used in the project instructions in this book; American terms, where these differ from British usage, are given in parentheses. The American term for 'miss' is 'skip', and 'tension' is known as 'gauge' in the US.

ch	chain	rem	remaining
dc	double crochet (single crochet)	tog	together
st(s)	stitch(es)	rep	repeat
cont	continue	sl st	slipstitch
beg	beginning	alt	alternate
htr	half treble (half double crochet)	approx	approximately
tr	treble (double crochet)	* or **	indicates stitches to be repeated;
dtr	double treble (treble crochet)	the number of repeats may be indicated in	
dec	decrease	brackets (parentheses)	
inc	increase		

MATERIALS

Where possible, I have included in the instructions the amount of yarn or thread required for each item. The main yarns used are:

- 1-ply acrylic
- DMC Fil à Dentelles no. 80 (equivalent to Coats no. 80)
- Twilley's Southern Comfort
- Moravia 40/2 Linen
- DMC 30s and 50s.

All of the following threads can be substituted for each other:

- Gütermann silk thread
- Madeira Tanne Cotona no. 30
- Mettler Stickgarn no. 30
- Colcoton Unikat 34/2.

See List of Suppliers, page 114.

Crochet hooks used are steel, nos. 1.75, 1.5, 1.25, 1.00, 0.75 and 0.60 (these are metric sizes, 0.60 being the finest). *Approximate* US equivalents are #4, #6, #8, #10, #12 and #14; but American sizes seem to vary from one manufacturer to another, so you should consult the manufacturer's literature to be sure.

Buttons and buttonholes

In such a small scale, I prefer not to use buttonholes. I favour instead sewing the garment onto the doll and using the buttons for decoration only. Buttons can be beads, bought miniature buttons, or home-made from polymer clay.

Skill levels

The following symbols are used to indicate the approximate degree of difficulty for each project:

easy   intermediate   experience needed

BABYWEAR

Everyone loves babies, and no miniature household would be complete without a cot in the nursery. The cot or pram blanket is one of the very easiest projects to make. This is followed by two simple designs to dress your baby girl or boy. As skill levels increase, try the carry-cape with its matching dress, or if you have a baby boy make the rompers instead. Babies have always looked cute in a pram set; this project, although fiddly to make, is well worth the effort involved. The final design in this chapter is the pièce de résistance, a christening outfit. It is a challenging project, not for the beginner, but it will become a treasured heirloom.

COT OR PRAM BLANKET

Materials

Small amounts of
one-ply yarn in
assorted colours

1.5mm (US #6)
crochet hook

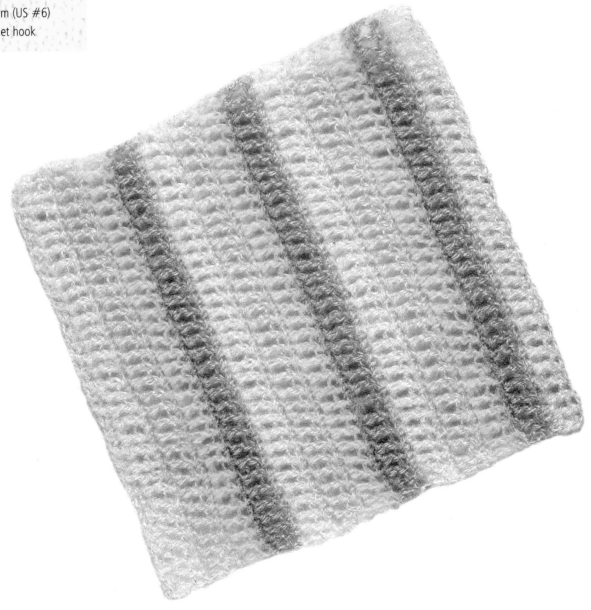

Make 31 ch, 1 dc in second ch from hook, 1 dc in each ch to end, 3 ch, turn.

Next row Miss first st, 1 tr in next dc, 1 tr in each dc to end, 1 tr in turning ch, 1 ch, turn.

* Change colour Miss first st, 1 dc in each tr to end, 1 dc in turning ch, 3 ch, turn.

Next row Miss first st, 1 tr in next dc, 1 tr in each dc to end, 1 tr in turning ch, 1 ch, turn. Rep from * 11 times more, ending with the first colour. Fasten off by passing the yarn through the final loop and cut.

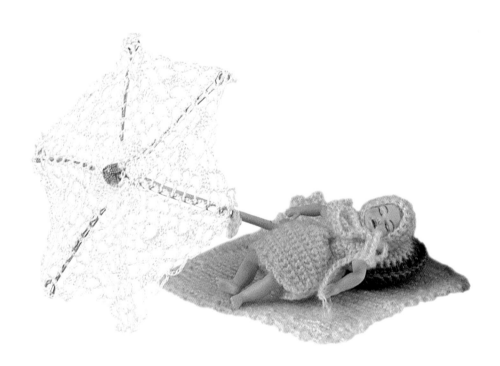

BABY BOY OUTFIT

Materials

One-ply yarn (approx. 60 metres)

1.00 and 1.25mm (US #10 and #8) crochet hooks

Tiny pompon for hat

JUMPER

Using 1.00mm (#10) crochet hook, make 11 ch, 1 dc in second ch from hook, 1 dc in each ch to end, 1 ch, turn (10 dc plus turning ch).

Next row Miss first st, 1 dc in next dc, 1 dc in each dc to end, 1 dc in turning ch, 1 ch, turn. Work 10 more rows in dc.

Next row Miss first st, 1 dc in next 2 dc, work 5 ch loosely, miss next 5 ch, 1 dc in next 2 dc, 1 dc in turning ch, 1 ch, turn.

Next row Miss first st, 1 dc in next 2 dc, 1 dc in each ch, 1 dc in next 2 dc, 1 dc in turning ch, 1 ch, turn.

Work 12 rows in dc. Fasten off.

Sleeves (make two)

Rejoin yarn with a sl st at the sixth row from the beginning, 1 ch, work 11 dc across armhole edge until sixth row from the second side, 1 ch, turn. Work six rows in dc.

Next row Miss first st, dc 2 tog across row, 1 dc in turning ch. Fasten off.

Sew up one side and sleeve seam, fit on doll and sew the second seam. Run a length of yarn through each wrist, pull up to fit, do the same around neck.

SHORTS

Using 1.00mm (#10) crochet hook, work 20 ch, 1 dc in second ch from hook, 1 dc in each ch to end, 1 ch, turn (19 dc plus turning ch). Work seven rows in dc. Fasten off.

Sew up back seam, join back and front together with a few stitches for the crotch. Fit on doll, run a length of yarn through top edge, pull up to fit.

HAT

Using 1.00mm (#10) crochet hook, work 4 ch, join into a ring with a sl st, 1 ch, 8 dc into ring, sl st to join.

Next row 1 ch, 1 dc into same st, * 2 dc into next dc; rep from *; sl st to join.

Next row 1 ch, 1 dc in each dc, sl st to join. Rep the last row four times more. Fasten off. Glue a tiny pompon to top.

SHAWL

Using 1.25mm (#8) crochet hook, make 35 ch, 1 dc in second ch from hook, 1 dc in each ch to end, 1 ch, turn (34 dc plus turning ch).

Next row Miss first st, 1 dc in next dc, * 2 ch, miss next dc, 1 dc in next dc; rep from * ending with 1 dc in turning ch, 1 ch, turn.

Next row Miss first st, 1 dc in next st, * 1 dc in 2 ch space, 1 dc in next dc, rep from * to end, ending with 1 dc in turning ch, 1 ch turn. Rep last two rows for length required.

Work a row of dc all round, working 3 dc in each corner, sl st to join, 4 ch.

Next row 1 dc into next 2 dc, * 3 ch, 1 dc into next 2 dc; rep from * all round, working 2 sts at each corner to keep the edging flat, sl st to join. Fasten off.

BABY GIRL OUTFIT

Materials

One-ply yarn (approx. 60 metres)

1.00 and 1.25mm (US #10 and #8) crochet hooks.

DRESS

Bodice

With 1.00mm (#10) crochet hook, make 11 ch, 1 dc in second ch from hook, 1 dc in each ch to end, 1 ch, turn (10 dc plus turning ch).

Next row Miss first st, 1 dc in each dc to end, 1 dc in turning ch, 1 ch, turn.

Work six more rows in dc.

Next row Miss first st, 1 dc in next dc, work 7 ch loosely, miss next 7 dc, 1 dc in next dc, 1 dc in turning ch, 1 ch, turn.

Next row Miss first st, 1 dc in next dc, 1 dc in each ch, 1 dc in next dc, 1 dc in turning ch, 1 ch, turn (10 dc plus turning ch).

Work six more rows in dc. Do not fasten off.

Skirt

1 dc in first st (inc made), 1 dc in next st, * 2 dc in next st (inc made), 1 dc in next st; rep from * across front and back bodice, 1 ch, turn (32 dc, plus turning ch).

Work 10 rows in dc, ending the last row with 4 ch.

Next row Miss first 2 sts, 1 dc in next dc, * 3 ch, miss 1 dc, 1 dc in next dc; rep from *, ending with 1 dc in turning ch. Fasten off.

Fit on doll and sew up the side seam.

PANTIES

With 1.00mm (#10) crochet hook, make 10 ch, 1 dc in second ch from hook, 1 dc in each ch to end, 1 ch, turn (9 dc plus turning ch).

Work five rows in dc.

Dec row Miss first st, 1 dc in next 8 dc, 1 ch, turn.

Rep last row three times more, working 1 dc less on each row (5 dc plus turning ch).

Work one row in dc.

Inc row 1 dc in first st (inc made), 1 dc in each dc to end (6 dc plus turning ch), 1 ch, turn.

Rep the last row three times (9 dc plus turning ch).

Work five rows in dc. Fasten off.

Sew up one side seam, fit on doll, sew the second seam.

BONNET

With 1.00mm (#10) crochet hook, make 14 ch, 1 dc in second ch from hook, * 2 ch, miss next ch, 1 dc in next ch; rep from * to end, 2 ch, turn.

Next row * 1 dc in 2 ch space, 2 ch; rep from *, ending with the last dc in top of turning ch, 2 ch, turn.

Rep the last row once more, ending the last rep with 1 ch, turn.

Next row 1 dc into each dc and 2 ch space, 1 ch, turn (13 dc plus turning ch).

Work two rows in dc.

Next row Miss first st, dc 2 tog six times across the row, 1 dc in turning ch. Fasten off.

Run yarn through back of bonnet, pull up tightly, sew back seam for approx 0.5cm (¼in).

Ties

Make 35 ch, join to ch edge of bonnet with a sl st, dc across row, work 35 ch. Fasten off.

Trim the ends of ties approximately 0.5cm (¼in), run a needle through ends to fluff into a mock tassel.

SHAWL

Using 1.25mm (#8) crochet hook, make 30 ch, 1 dc in second ch from hook, 1 dc in each ch to end, 1 ch, turn (29 dc plus turning ch).

Next row Miss first st, 1 dc in each dc to end, 1 dc in turning ch, 1 ch, turn.

Rep last row 35 times, ending with 3 dc in turning ch.

Work a row of dc around the three remaining sides, working 3 dc at each corner.

Edging

Work 3 ch, 1 tr in next dc, 3 ch 1 htr around stem of last tr made, miss next dc, * 1 tr into next 2 dc, 3 ch 1 htr around stem of last tr made, miss next st; rep from *; sl st to join.

NB: when working the edging, omit the 'miss next dc' at corners, so the edging lies flat.

11 CARRY-CAPE AND ROMPERS OR DRESS

ALL-IN-ONE ROMPER OR DRESS AND ATTACHED PANTIES

Materials

½-ply yarn (approx. 100 metres), or two reels of Gütermann silk thread

0.60mm (US #14) crochet hook

2mm (1⁄16in) silk ribbon for ties

ROMPER OR DRESS BODICE AND PANTIES

Make 19 ch, 1 dc in second ch from hook, 1 dc in each ch to end, 1 ch, turn (18 dc plus turning ch). Work 13 rows in dc, or length required to measure from crotch to armhole, ending the last row with 2 ch, turn (for sleeve).

Next row 1 dc in second ch from hook, dc to end, 1 dc in turning ch, 2 ch, turn.

Rep the last row once more, ending with 1 ch, turn (22 dc plus turning ch).

Work 10 rows in dc.

Neck Miss first st, 1 dc in next 4 dc, make 13 ch, miss next 13 dc, 1 dc in next 4 dc, 1 dc in turning ch, 1 ch, turn.

Next row Miss first st, 1 dc in next 4 dc, 1 dc in each ch, 1 dc in next 4 dc, 1 dc in turning ch, 1 ch, turn.

Work nine rows in dc (22 dc plus turning ch).

Next row Miss first st, 1 dc in next 20 dc, 1 ch, turn.

Next row Miss first st, 1 dc in next 18 dc, 1 ch, turn.

Work 13 rows in dc. Fasten off.

With right side facing, rejoin yarn with a sl st to sleeve edge, work one row in dc. Fasten off. Rep on second sleeve.

Slip over doll's head, sew up side seams, close neck a little more with a few sts, work a few sts to close the crotch. This completes the rompers.

Skirt for dress (if required)

Make 64 ch.

Foundation row 1 tr in fourth ch from hook, (1 tr, 1 ch, 1 tr) into next ch, * miss 2 ch, 3 tr in next ch, miss 2 ch, (1 tr, 1 ch, 1 tr) in next ch; rep from *, ending with miss 2 ch, 3 tr in next ch, 1 tr in last ch, 3 ch, turn.

First pattern row * Miss first 2 sts, 3 tr into centre of next 3 tr group, (1 tr, 1 ch, 1 tr) into next 1 ch space; rep from *, ending with 1 tr in turning ch, 3 ch, turn.

Second pattern row * (1 tr, 1 ch, 1 tr) in next ch space, 3 tr in centre of 3 tr group; rep from *, ending with 1 tr in turning ch, 3 ch, turn.

Rep the two pattern rows 10 times, or to length required. Fasten off.

Sew up the back seam, run a gathering thread through top of skirt, pull up to fit, sl st to the bodice.

HOODED CARRY-CAPE

Make 26 ch, 1 dc in second ch from hook, 1 dc in each ch to end, 1 ch, turn.

Next row Miss first st, dc to end, 1 dc in turning ch, 1 ch, turn.

Work 15 more rows in dc, or until the work measures from top of head to neck.

Next row Miss first st, 1 dc in next dc, * 3 ch, miss next dc, 1 dc in next 2 dc; rep from *, ending with 1 dc in last dc, 1 dc in turning ch, 1 ch, turn.

Next row Miss first st, 1 dc in next dc, * 1 dc in 3 ch space, 1 dc in next 2 dc; rep from *, ending with 1 dc in 3 ch space, 1 dc in last dc, 1 dc in turning ch, 3 ch, turn.

Inc row 1 tr in first st, 2 tr in each st, ending with 1 tr in turning ch, 3 ch, turn (50 tr plus turning ch).

Work one row in trebles.

Rep the last two rows once more (100 tr plus turning ch).

Foundation row Miss first st, (1 tr, 1 ch, 1 tr) in next tr, * miss 2 tr, 3 tr in next tr, miss 2 tr, (1 tr, 1 ch, 1 tr) in next tr; rep from *, ending with 1 tr in turning ch, 3 ch, turn.

Pattern row (1 tr, 1 ch, 1 tr) in 1 ch space, * 3 tr in centre of 3 tr group, (1 tr, 1 ch, 1 tr) in 1 ch space; rep from *, ending with 1 tr in turning ch, 3 ch, turn.

Rep pattern row 21 times, or to length required. Fasten off.

Fold the hood in half and sew across the top seam. Thread ribbon or length of chain through the holes at neck.

PRAM SET

LEGGINGS (make two)

Make 18 ch, 1 dc in second ch from hook, 1 dc in each ch to end, 1 ch, turn (17 dc plus turning ch).

Work 25 rows in dc, or until length measures from waist to bottom of foot.

Dec row Miss first st, dc 2 tog across row, 1 dc in turning ch, 1 ch, turn.

Work one row in dc.

Work dec row once more. Fasten off.

Measure against doll, mark the crotch, sew up front and half the back seam, sew up leg seams, fit on doll, sew up rest of the back seam. Run a gathering thread through waist, pull up to fit.

JACKET

Make 18 ch, 1 dc in second ch from hook, 1 dc in each ch to end, 1 ch, turn (17 dc plus turning ch). Work eight rows in dc.

Next row Miss first st, 1 dc in next 14 dc, 1 ch, turn.

Next row Miss first st, 1 dc in next 11 dc, 1 ch, turn.

Work six rows in dc.

Next row Miss first st, 1 dc in next 2 dc, 1 ch, turn.

Work two rows in dc, working 5 ch at end of the last row, turn.

Next row 1 dc in second ch from hook, 1 dc in next 3 ch, 1 dc in each dc to end, 1 dc in turning ch, 1 ch, turn.

Work six rows in dc, working 3 ch at end of the last row.

Next row 1 dc in second ch from hook, 1 dc in next ch, dc to end.

Work nine rows in dc. Fasten off.

Miss the next 6 dc at the neck edge, rejoin thread with a sl st, 1 ch, 1 dc in next st, 1 dc in turning ch, 1 ch, turn.

Work one row in dc, working 5 ch at end of row.

Next row 1 dc in second ch from hook, 1 dc in next 3 ch, 1 dc in next 2 dc, 1 dc in turning ch, 1 ch, turn.

Work six rows in dc, working 3 ch at end of last row, turn.

Next row 1 dc in second ch from hook, 1 dc in next ch, dc to end, 1 ch, turn. Work nine rows in dc. Fasten off.

Sleeves (make two)

Rejoin thread to armhole edge with a sl st, 1 ch, work 15 dc across armhole, 1 ch, turn.

Work 10 rows in dc, decreasing 1 st at each end of the fifth and ninth rows (11 dc, plus turning ch). Fasten off.

Sew up side and sleeve seams.

Collar

Missing the first 4 sts at the front neck edge, rejoin thread with a sl st, 1 ch, work 22 dc around neck, ending 4 sts from the second front edge.

** Work one row in dc.

Inc row Work in dc, working twice into second and second last sts. Rep from ** once more. Fasten off.

Sew on tiny seed beads for buttons.

BONNET

Make 24 ch, 1 dc in second ch from hook, 1 dc in each ch to end, 1 ch, turn (23 dc plus turning ch). Work eight rows in dc.

First dec row Miss first st, dc 2 tog across row, 1 dc in turning ch, 1 ch, turn.

Second dec row Miss first st, dc 2 tog across row, end with dc the last st and turning ch tog, 1 ch, turn.

Rep the first dec row once more. Fasten off.

Gather the back edge, sew up seam for 0.5cm (¼in), add ribbon ties.

Materials

Two 300m reels
of DMC Broder
Machine 30

0.60mm (US #14)
crochet hook

2mm (¹⁄₁₆in) silk ribbon

Miniature nappy
(diaper) pin

NAPPY (DIAPER)

Top edge Make 30 ch, 1 dc in second ch from hook, 1 dc in each ch, 1 ch, turn (29 dc plus turning ch).

Work five rows in dc.

Next row Miss first st, 1 dc in next 22 dc, 1 ch, turn.

Next row Miss first st, 1 dc in next 15 dc, 1 ch, turn.

Work two rows in dc.

First dec row Miss first st, dc 2 tog, dc to end, 1 dc in turning ch, 1 ch, turn.

Rep the dec row seven times more (7 dc plus turning ch).

Work in dc for approx 2cm (¾in). Fasten off.

Lay the doll on the nappy, placing the narrow strip between the legs, sew through all pieces at the front. Sew on nappy pin if required.

DRESS

Bodice

Make 16 ch, 1 dc in second ch from hook, 1 dc in each ch to end, 1 ch, turn (15 dc plus turning ch).

Work two rows in dc.

Next row Miss first st, 1 dc in next 13 dc, 1 ch, turn.

Next row Miss first st, 1 dc in next 11 dc, 1 ch, turn.

Work seven rows in dc.

Divide for neck

Next row Miss first st, 1 dc in the next 2 dc, 1 ch, turn.

Work two more rows in dc, working 4 ch at end of second row for back neck edge.

** **Next row** 1 dc in second ch from hook, 1 dc in next 2 ch, dc to end of row, 1 ch, turn (6 dc plus turning ch).

Work six rows in dc, working 2 ch at end of last row.

Next row 1 dc in second ch from hook, dc to end, 1 ch, turn (8 dc plus turning ch).
Work 3 rows in dc. Fasten off. **
Return to neck edge, miss next 6 dc, rejoin thread to next dc with a sl st, 1 ch, dc to end, 1 ch, turn. Work three rows in dc working 4 ch at end of row, turn.
Rep from ** to **.

Sleeves (make two)

Rejoin thread to armhole edge with a sl st, 1 ch, work 32 dc across armhole, 1 ch, turn.

Foundation row Miss first st, 1 dc in next st, * 2 ch, miss next st, 1 dc in next st; rep from *, working last dc in turning ch, 1 ch, turn.

Pattern row 1 dc in first 2 ch space, * 2 ch, 1 dc in next 2 ch space; rep from *, ending with 1 dc in turning ch, 1 ch, turn.

Rep pattern row nine times more, or to length required.

Next row Work 1 dc in each 2 ch space. Fasten off.

Sew up the side seams and half the sleeve seam. Work a row of double crochet around neck.

Underskirt

Starting at back waist edge, rejoin thread with a sl st, 1 ch, 1 dc in same st. Work 60 dc across waist edge, 1 ch, turn.

Work pattern as on sleeve for approximately 25 rows, or to length required, end last row with 3 ch, turn.

Edging

Work 3 tr in first ch space, * miss next 2 ch space, 5 tr in next 2 ch space; rep from *, ending with 3 tr in turning ch. Fasten off.

Sew up half the back seam, fit on doll and sew up the rest of the back and sleeve seams. Run a length of thread through wrist edge, pull up to fit.

Overskirt

Make 71 ch, 1 dc in second ch from hook, 1 dc in each ch to end, 3 ch, turn.

Foundation row Miss first st, 1 tr in next dc, 1 ch, miss 2 dc, * 3 tr in next dc, 1 ch, miss 2 dc, 1 tr in next dc, 1 ch, miss 2 dc; rep from *, ending with 3 tr in turning ch, 3 ch, turn.

First pattern row 1 tr in first tr, * 1 ch, 3 tr in single tr, 1 ch, 1 tr in centre of 3 tr group; rep from *, ending with 1 ch, 2 tr in last tr, 1 tr in turning ch, 3 ch, turn.

Second pattern row Miss first st, 1 tr in next st, * 1 ch, 3 tr in single tr, 1 ch, 1 tr in centre of 3 tr group; rep from *, ending with 1 ch, 3 tr in last tr, 3 ch, turn.

Rep the two pattern rows once more.

Next row 3 tr in second tr, * 1 ch, 3 tr in single tr, 1 ch, 3 tr in centre of 3 tr group; rep from *, ending with 3 tr in last tr, 1 tr in turning ch, 4 ch, turn.

Pattern row * 3 tr in 3 tr group, 1 ch; rep from * to end, 1 tr in turning ch, 4 ch, turn.

Rep the pattern row until the work measures the same length as the underskirt minus the edging, working only 1 turning ch on the last row.

Shell edging

Work 5 tr in centre of 3 tr group, 1 dc in 1 ch space; rep from *, ending with 1 dc in turning ch. Fasten off.

BONNET

Make 6 ch, join into a ring with a sl st, 1 ch, 8 dc into ring, sl st to join.

Next row 1 ch, 1 dc in same st, 2 dc in each dc, sl st to join.

Next row 1 ch, 1 dc in same st, * 1 dc in next dc, 2 dc in next dc; rep from *, sl st to join.

Rep last row once more, working 3 ch at end of row.

Foundation row 1 tr in same st as 3 ch, miss 2 dc, * 1 ch, 3 tr in next dc, 1 ch, miss next 2 dc, 1 tr in next dc; rep from * ending with 1 ch, miss 2 dc, 3 tr in next dc, 1 ch, 2 tr in last st, 3 ch, turn.

First pattern row 2 tr in first st, * 1 ch, 1 tr in 3 tr group, 1 ch, 3 tr in single tr; rep from *, ending with 2 tr in last tr, 1 tr in turning ch, 3 ch, turn.

Second pattern row 1 tr in first st, * 1 ch, 3 tr in single tr, 1 ch, 1 tr in 3 tr group; rep from *, ending with 1 ch, 3 tr in single tr, 1 ch, 2 tr in last tr, 3 ch, turn.

Rep the two pattern rows once. Fasten off.

Sew up back of bonnet for approx 0.5cm (¼in), sew on ribbon ties.

SHAWL

Make 76 ch.

Foundation row 1 tr into fourth ch from hook, 1 ch, miss 2 ch, * 3 tr in next ch, 1 ch, miss 2 ch, 1 tr in next ch, 1 ch, miss 2 ch; rep from *, ending with 2 tr in last ch, 3 ch, turn.

First pattern row 2 tr in first tr, * 1 ch, 1 tr in centre 3 tr group, 1 ch, 3 tr in single tr; rep from *, ending with 2 tr in last tr, 3 ch, turn.

Second pattern row 1 tr in first tr, * 1 ch, 3 tr in single tr, 1 ch, 1 tr in centre of 3 tr group; rep from *, ending with 1 tr in last tr, 3 ch, turn.

Rep the two pattern rows 13 times, working 1 turning ch on the last row.

* Work 55 dc across edge, work 3 dc in the corner st; rep from * all the way round, join to first dc with a sl st.

Shell border

3 ch, 4 tr in corner st, 1 dc in next dc, * miss 1 dc, 5 tr in next dc, miss 1 dc, 1 dc in next dc; rep from * all round edge.

Note: omit the 'miss next dc' at each corner so the edging lies flat. Fasten off.

2

CHILDRENSWEAR

In this chapter I have designed items of clothing for both boys and girls. Of course, the boys' items can be used for little girls also. Children's fashions have not changed a great deal over the last 80 years. Where they do vary is in the choice of colours – children since the 1960s do appear to have been dressed far more colourfully than those from an earlier era. The last two designs would be equally suitable for children from Victorian times or from a more recent period.

① BOY'S JUMPER, SHORTS AND BOBBLE HAT

Materials

One-ply yarn in two colours (approx 20 metres of A, 10m of B)

Small pompon

1.25mm (US #8) crochet hook

JUMPER

Using colour A, make 14 ch, 1 dc in second ch from hook, 1 dc in each ch to end, 1 ch, turn. Work 17 rows in dc.

Next row Miss first st, 1 dc in next 2 dc, 8 ch, miss 8 dc, dc to end, 1 dc in turning ch, 1 ch, turn.

Next row Miss first st, 1 dc in next 2 dc, 1 dc in each ch, dc to end, 1 dc in turning ch, 1 ch, turn. Work 18 rows in dc. Fasten off.

Collar (if required)

Starting at centre front and working all around neck to centre front, work five rows in dc. **NB:** Turn after each row for an open collar, or work in rounds for a polo (turtleneck) collar.

Sleeves (make two)

Make 16 ch, 1 dc in second ch from hook, 1 dc in each ch to end, 1 ch, turn. Work 10 rows in dc.

Cuff

Miss first st, work 2 dc tog across row, ending with 1 dc in turning ch, 1 ch, turn. Work two more rows in dc. Fasten off. Sew sleeve to jumper, sew up side seams, catch down ends of collar.

SHORTS

Using B, make 14 ch, 1 dc in each ch to end, 1 ch, turn. Work 13 rows in dc. Fasten off. Make another piece to match. Place both pieces right sides together and sew back and front seams to halfway mark. Sew leg seams across. Fit on the doll, run a gathering thread through waist edge, pull up to fit. Fasten off.

BOBBLE HAT

Using B, make 20 ch, 1 dc in second ch from hook, 1 dc in each ch, 1 ch, turn. Work three rows in dc. **Dec row** Miss first st, 1 dc in next st, * dc 2 tog, 1 dc; rep from *, ending with 1 dc in turning ch, 1 ch, turn. Rep the dec row once more. Work one more row in dc. Draw yarn through sts and pull up tight. Fasten off. Add a pompon to top.

BOY'S COAT AND CAP

9cm (3½in) doll

Materials

One-ply yarn (approx. 50 metres)

1.25mm (US #8) crochet hook

Tiny buttons or beads

COAT

Back and fronts

Make 19 ch, 1 dc in second ch from hook, 1 dc in each ch to end, 1 ch, turn.

Work four rows in dc, omitting 1 ch, turn on the last row. Break yarn.

Work a second piece but do not break yarn. Work one row in dc, omitting the 1 ch, turn. Work across the first piece, ending 1 ch, turn.

Work 12 rows in dc.

Divide for armholes

Right front Miss first st, 1 dc in next 8 dc, 1 ch, turn.

Work eight rows in dc.

Neck shaping Miss first st, 1 dc in next 4 dc, 1 ch, turn.

Work two rows in dc for the shoulder. Fasten off.

Back Return to the main section. Miss next 3 dc, rejoin yarn to next dc with a sl st, 1 ch, 1 dc in next 13 dc, 1 ch, turn.

Work 12 more rows in dc. Fasten off.

Left front Return to main piece, miss next 3 dc, rejoin yarn to next dc with a sl st, dc to end, 1 dc in turning ch, 1 ch, turn.

Work seven rows in dc.

Neck shaping Miss first st, 1 dc in next 4 dc, 1 ch, turn.

Work three rows in dc. Fasten off. Sew up shoulder seams.

Collar

Miss first 2 sts at neck edge, rejoin yarn to next st with a sl st, 1 ch, work 26 dc across the neck edge, ending with 1 dc in the third last st, 1 ch, turn.

Work one row in dc.

Next row 1 dc in first st (inc st), dc to end, work 2 dc in last dc, 1 dc in turning ch, 1 ch, turn.

Work one row in dc. Fasten off.

Sleeves (make two)

Make 16 ch, 1 dc in second ch from hook, 1 dc in each ch to end, 1 ch, turn (15 dc plus turning ch).

Next row Miss first st, 1 dc in each dc, 1 dc in turning ch, 1 ch, turn.

Work one row in dc.

Inc row 1 dc in first st (inc made), 1 dc in each dc working twice into last dc (inc made), 1 dc in turning ch, 1 ch, turn (17 dc plus turning ch).

* Work two rows in dc.

Rep the inc row (19 dc plus turning ch).

Rep from * twice more (23 dc plus turning ch).

Work four rows in dc. Fasten off.

Sew up the side seam, set sleeve into the armhole.

Sew on tiny buttons or beads.

CAP

Make 4 ch, join into a ring with a sl st. Work 1 ch, 7 dc into ring, sl st to join.

Next row 1 ch, 1 dc into first st, 2 dc in next and every dc all round, sl st to join (15 dc plus ch).

Next row 1 ch, 1 dc in each dc, sl st to join.

Next row 1 ch, 1 dc in same st, * 1 dc in next dc, 2 dc in next dc; rep from *, sl st to join.

Rep last row twice more.

Next row 1 ch, work 1 dc in next 10 dc, 1 ch, turn.

Next row Miss first dc, 1 dc in next 9 dc, 1 ch, turn.

Next row Miss first dc, 1 dc in next 8 dc, 1 ch, turn.

Next row Miss first dc, 1 dc in next 7 dc, 1 ch, turn.

Work a row of dc all round cap, sl st to join. Fasten off.

BOY'S SHIRT, TROUSERS AND JUMPER

9cm (3½in) doll

SHIRT

Back

Using DMC 30s, make 20 ch, 1 dc in second ch from hook, 1 dc in each ch to end, 1 ch, turn (19 dc plus turning ch).

Work 12 rows in dc.

Next row Miss first st, 1 dc in next 16 dc, 1 ch, turn.

Next row Miss first st, 1 dc in next 13 dc, 1 ch, turn.

Work 14 rows in dc.

Shoulder Miss first st, 1 dc in next 3 dc, 1 ch, turn.

Next row Miss first st, 1 dc in next 2 dc, 1 dc in turning ch, 1 ch, turn.

Rep the last row three times more, ending with 6 ch on the last row, turn.

** Right front

1 dc in second ch from hook, 1 dc in next 4 ch, dc to end (8 dc plus turning ch).

Next row Work 12 rows in dc, working 4 ch at the end of the last row, turn.

Next row 1 dc in second ch from hook, 1 dc in next 2 ch, dc to end working 1 dc in turning ch, 1 ch, turn (12 dc plus turning ch).

Work 11 rows in dc. Fasten off. **

Left shoulder and front

Return to neck edge, miss next 6 dc, rejoin thread to next dc with a sl st, 1 ch, 1 dc, in next 2 dc, 1 dc in turning ch, 1 ch, turn.

Next row Miss first st, 1 dc in next 2 dc, 1 dc in turning ch, 1 ch, turn.

Rep the last row twice more, ending with 6 ch on the second row, turn.

Work from ** to ** as for the right front.

Materials

Small amount of white DMC 30s for shirt

One ball of DMC Fil à Dentelles 80 in colour A for trousers and jumper

Small amount of DMC Fil à Dentelles 80 in B for the jumper

0.60mm (US #14) crochet hook

Tiny beads or buttons

Sleeves (make two)

Rejoin thread at the armhole edge with a sl st, 1 ch, work 31 dc across armhole edge, 1 ch, turn. Work one row in dc.

Dec row Miss first st, 1 dc in next dc, work 2 dc tog, dc to end, 1 dc in turning ch, 1 ch, turn.

Rep the last row until there are 21 sts left.

Work seven rows in dc.

Cuff

Miss first st, 1 dc in next dc, work 2 dc tog across the row, 1 dc in last dc, 1 dc, in turning ch, 1 ch, turn (12 dc plus turning ch).

Work four rows in dc. Fasten off.

Collar

Return to right front neck edge, miss the first 3 sts, work 26 dc across neck edge, ending 3 sts from the left front edge, 1 ch, turn.

Next row 1 dc in first st (inc made), dc to last dc, dc twice into this st (inc made), 1 dc in turning ch, 1 ch, turn.

Rep the last row four times more. Fasten off. Sew up side seams and half of each sleeve seam, fit on doll, sew up rest of sleeves. Overlap the fronts and lightly tack down, sew on buttons or beads.

TROUSERS

Right leg

Using DMC Fil à Dentelles 80 in colour A, make 20 ch, 1 dc in second ch from hook, 1 dc in each dc to end, 1 ch, turn (19 dc plus turning ch).

Work four rows in dc.

** **Next row** Miss first st, 1 dc in next 9 dc, 1 ch, turn.

Next row Miss first st, dc to end, 1 dc in turning ch, 1 ch, turn.

Next row Miss first st, 1 dc in next 8 dc, 1 dc in turning ch, 1 ch, turn.

Next row Miss first st, dc to end, 1 dc in turning ch, 1 ch, turn. **

Work 11 rows in dc, working 2 ch at the end of the last row, turn.

*** **Next row** 1 dc in second ch from hook, 1 dc in each dc to end, 1 dc in turning ch, 2 ch, turn.

Rep the last row once more, ending with 1 ch, turn (23 dc plus turning ch).

Work 20 more rows in dc. Fasten off. ***

Left leg

Work 20 ch, 1 dc in second ch from hook, 1 dc in each dc to end, 1 ch, turn (19 dc plus turning ch).

Work five rows in dc.

Rep from ** to ** as for the right leg.

Work 10 rows in dc, working 2 ch at the end of the last row, turn.

Work from *** to *** as for the right leg.

Sew up the front seam (shorter side is the front), and half the back seam. Sew up leg seams. Fit on doll, sew up the rest of the back seam. Run two separate lengths of thread through waist, pull up to fit.

STRIPED JUMPER

Using DMC Fil à Dentelles 80 in A, make 22 ch, 1 dc in second ch from hook, 1 dc in each ch to end, 1 ch, turn (21 dc plus turning ch).

Work three rows in dc; work two rows in B, and four rows in A; rep the last six rows three times.

Next row Miss first st, 1 dc in next 5 dc, 1 ch, turn.

Work four rows in dc. Fasten off.

Return to neck edge, miss the next 10 dc, rejoin thread with a sl st to next dc, 1 ch, 1 dc in each dc to end, 1 dc in turning ch, 1 ch, turn.

Work four rows in dc.

Next row Miss first st, 1 dc in next 5 dc, work 10 ch, work across the dc on the first shoulder, 1 dc in turning ch, 1 ch, turn.

Next row Miss first st, 1 dc in next 5 dc, 1 dc in each of the 10 ch, 1 dc in turning ch on second shoulder, 1 dc in each dc to end, 1 dc in turning ch, 1 ch, turn (21 dc plus turning ch). Work three rows in dc.

Change to colour B, work two rows in dc; change to colour A, work four rows in dc. Rep the last six rows to match the front. Fasten off.

Measure against the doll and mark armhole, work
three rows in dc across armhole. Fasten off. Work
a row of dc around neck edge. Sew up one side
seam, fit on doll, sew up the second side seam.

Note: When changing colour, half-work the dc in
the turning ch in the old colour, work the second
half of the stitch in the new colour, 1 ch, turn.
Start the next row using the new colour.

⑪ GIRL'S LONG-SLEEVED DRESS & HAT

7.5cm (3in) doll

Materials

One-ply yarn, approx. 50 metres

1.25mm (US #8) crochet hook

Flowers or ribbons as required

DRESS

Make 12 ch, 1 dc in second ch from hook, 1 dc in each ch to end, 1 ch, turn (11 dc plus turning ch).

Next row Miss first st, 1 dc in each dc to end, 1 dc in turning ch 1 ch, turn.

Work nine rows in dc.

Shape for neck Miss first st, 1 dc in next 2 dc, 6 ch, miss next 6 dc, dc in next 2 dc 1 dc in turning ch, 1 ch, turn.

Next row Miss first st, 1 dc in next 2 dc, 1 dc in each ch, 1 dc in next 2 dc, 1 dc in turning ch, 1 ch, turn. Work 10 rows in dc. Fasten off.

Sleeves (make two)

Make 16 ch. 1 dc in second ch from hook, 1 dc in each ch to end, 1 ch, turn.

Work eight rows in dc.

Cuff

Dec row Miss first st, * dc 2 tog, 1 dc; rep from *, ending with 1 dc in turning ch. Work one row in dc. Fasten off. Set in sleeves, sew up side and sleeve seams.

Skirt

With wrong side facing, starting at centre back rejoin yarn with a sl st, 1 ch, 1 dc in same st, 2 dc in each st, 1 ch, turn (47 dc plus turning ch).

Next row Miss first dc, 1 dc in each dc to end, 3 ch, turn.

First pattern row Miss first 2 sts, 1 tr in next dc, 1 tr in second missed dc, * miss next dc, 1 tr in next dc, 1 tr in missed dc; rep from * to end of row, ending with 1 tr in last st, 1 ch, turn.

Second pattern row Miss first tr, 1 dc in each tr to end, 3 ch, turn.

Rep the two pattern rows twice more, then first row once more. Fasten off and sew up back skirt seam.

HAT

Make 3 ch, join into a ring with a sl st, 1 ch, work 5 dc into ring, sl st to join.

Next row 1 ch, 1 dc in same space, 2 dc in each dc to end, sl st to join.

Rep last row once more.

Next row 1 ch, 1 dc in each dc to end, sl st to join. Rep the last row five times more.

Next row 1 ch, 1 dc in same space, 2 dc in each dc to end, sl st to join.

Next row 3 ch, * miss first dc, 1 tr in next dc, 1 tr in missed dc; rep from *, ending with a sl st into top of 3 ch. Fasten off.

Stiffen with spray starch or dilute white PVA glue. Add flowers or ribbons as required.

GIRL'S DRESS, PANTALOONS AND HAT

6.5–7.5cm (2½–3in) doll

PANTALOONS (Make 2 pieces)

Make 20 ch, 1 dc in second ch from hook, 1 dc in each ch to end, 1 ch, turn.

Work 13 rows in dc, working 2 ch at the end of the last row, turn.

Next row 1 dc in second ch from hook, dc to end, 2 ch, turn.

Next row 1 dc in second ch from hook, dc to end, 1 ch, turn.

Work five rows in dc, ending with 3 ch on the last row.

Edging

Miss first st, 1 tr in next st, 3 ch, 1 htr around stem of last tr, * 1 tr in next 2 sts, 3 ch, 1 htr around stem of last tr; rep from * ending with 1 tr in last st, 1 tr in turning ch. Fasten off.

Sew up front and leg seams, fit on doll, sew up the back seam. Run a length of thread through waist, pull up to fit.

DRESS

Bodice

Make 18 ch, 1 dc in second ch from hook, 1 dc in each ch to end, 1 ch, turn.

Work two rows in dc.

Next row Miss first st, 1 dc in next 14 dc, 1 ch, turn

Next row Miss first st, 1 dc in next 11 dc, 1 ch, turn.

Work five rows in dc.

Next row Miss first st, 1 dc in next 2 dc, 1 ch, turn.

Work four rows in dc, working 3 ch at the end of the last row, turn.

Next row 1 dc in second ch from hook, 1 dc in next ch, dc to end, 1 ch, turn (5 dc plus turning ch). Work four rows in dc, working 4 ch at the end of the last row, turn.

Next row 1 dc in second ch from hook, 1 dc in next 2 ch, dc to end, 1 ch, turn (9 dc plus turning ch).

Work two rows in dc. Fasten off.

Return to neck edge, miss the next 6 dc, rejoin thread to next dc with a sl st, 1 ch, 1 dc in next dc, 1 dc in turning ch, 1 ch, turn.

Work five rows in dc, ending the last row with 3 ch, turn.

Materials

One 200m reel of Madeira Tanne Cotona no. 30

0.60mm (US #14) crochet hook

Ribbon for hat

Next row 1 dc in second ch from hook, 1 dc in next ch, dc to end, 1 ch, turn.

Work five rows in dc, ending the last row with 4 ch, turn.

Next row 1 dc in second ch from hook, 1 dc in next 2 ch, dc to end, 1 ch, turn (9 dc plus turning ch).

Work two rows in dc. Fasten off.

Sleeves (make two)

Rejoin thread at armhole edge with a sl st, 1 ch, work 20 dc across armhole, 1 ch, turn.

Next row Miss first st, 1 dc in next 4 dc, 2 dc in each of next 11 dc, 1 dc in next 4 dc, 1 dc in turning ch, 1 ch, turn.

Work seven rows in dc.

Next row Miss first st, 1 dc in next dc, dc 2 tog 14 times, 1 dc in next dc, 1 dc in turning ch, 1 ch, turn.

Work two rows in dc, ending the last row with 3 ch. Work edging as on pantaloons.

Skirt

Rejoin yarn to back edge of bodice with a sl st, 1 ch, work 73 dc across the fronts and back, 3 ch, turn.

Next row Miss first st, 1 tr in next dc, * miss 2 dc, ([1 tr, 1 ch,] 3 times, 1 tr) in next dc (one shell made); rep from *, ending with 1 tr, 1 ch, 1 tr in last st, 4 ch, turn.

Next row 1 tr in 1 ch space, * ([1 tr, 1 ch,] 3 times, 1 tr) in centre space of shell; rep from *, ending with 1 tr, 1 ch, 1 tr in last 1 ch, space, 4 ch, turn.

Rep the last row eight times. Fasten off.

Work a row of dc around neck edge.

Fit on doll, sew up back seam. Run a gathering thread through waist, pull up to fit, do the same with the puff sleeves, running the gathering thread just above the edging.

HAT

Make 4 ch, join into a ring with a sl st, 1 ch,

work 8 dc into ring, sl st to join.

Next row 1 ch, 1 dc in same st; 2 dc in each dc to end, sl st to join.

Next row 1 ch, 1 dc in same st, * 1 dc in next dc, 2 dc in next dc; rep from *; sl st to join.

Next row 1 ch, 1 dc in same st, * 1 dc in next 2 dc, 2 dc in next dc; rep from *; sl st to join.

Rep last row once more, ending with 1 dc in last 2 dc, sl st to join.

Next row 1 ch, miss first st, 1 dc in next and every dc, sl st to join.

Rep last row five times more.

Next row 1 ch, 1 dc in same st, 1 dc in next dc, * 2 dc in next dc, 1 dc in next dc; rep from * sl st to join.

Next row 1 ch, miss first st, 1 dc in each dc, sl st to join.

Next row 4 ch, ([1 tr, 1 ch] twice, 1 tr) in same st, * miss 2 dc, ([1 tr, 1 ch] 3 times, 1 tr) in next dc; rep from *; miss last 2 dc, sl st to centre ch of shell.

Next row 4 ch, ([1 tr, 1 ch] twice, 1 tr) in same shell, * ([1 tr, 1 ch] 3 times, 1 tr) in centre of next shell; rep from *, ending with a sl st in third of 4 ch to join. Fasten off.

Stiffen with spray starch or dilute white PVA glue. Decorate as required.

⑪ BRIDESMAID'S OUTFIT

10cm (4in) doll

PANTIES

Starting at the front top edge, make 17 ch, 1 dc in second ch from hook, 1 dc in each ch to end, 1 ch, turn (16 dc plus turning ch).

Work five rows in dc.

Next row Miss first st, dc 2 tog, dc to last 2 dc, dc 2 tog, 1 dc in turning ch, 1 ch, turn.

Rep the last row four times (6 dc plus turning ch). Work 10 rows in dc.

Inc row 1 dc in first st (inc made), 1 dc in next dc, 2 dc in each of next 2 dc, 1 dc in next dc, 2 dc in next dc, 1 dc in turning ch, 1 ch, turn (10 dc plus turning ch).

Work one row in dc.

Next row 1 dc in first st (inc made), dc to last st, 2 dc in this st, 1 dc in turning ch, 1 ch, turn.

Work one row in dc.

Rep the last inc row three times more.

Work six rows in dc. Fasten off.

Fit on doll, sew up the side seams, run a length of thread through the waist edge, pull up to fit.

DRESS

Bodice

Make 15 ch, 1 dc in second ch from hook, 1 dc in each ch to end, 1 ch, turn (14 dc plus turning ch).

Work three rows in dc.

Inc row Miss first st, * 1 dc in next dc, 2 dc in next dc; rep from * 5 times more, 1 dc in next dc, 1 dc in turning ch, 1 ch, turn.

Work two rows in dc.

Divide for armhole Miss first st, 1 dc in next 18 dc, 1 ch, turn.

Next row Miss first st, 1 dc in next 16 dc, 1 ch, turn.

Work four rows in dc.

Divide for neck Miss first st, 1 dc in next 3 dc, 1 ch, turn.

Work 10 rows in dc, working 4 ch, at the end of the last row, turn.

** **Next row** 1 dc in second ch from hook, 1 dc in next 2 ch, 1 dc in each dc to end, 1 ch, turn.

Work four rows in dc, ending last row with 3 ch, turn.

Next row 1 dc in second ch from hook, 1 dc in next ch, dc to end, 1 ch, turn.

Work six rows in dc, decreasing 2 sts on the third row. Fasten off. **

Return to neck edge, miss the next 9 dc, rejoin yarn with a sl st to next dc, 1 ch, dc to end, 1 ch, turn.

Materials

Small amount of DMC Broder Machine 30 in white for the panties

One reel of Madeira Tanne/Cotona 30 for the dress and hat

0.60mm (US #14) crochet hook

Silk ribbon and rose

Work nine rows in dc, working 4 ch, at end of last row, turn.

Rep from ** to ** as on first front.

Sleeves (make two)

These are worked at the armhole rather than sewn on later.

Rejoin thread to armhole edge with a sl st, 1 ch, work 25 dc across armhole, 1 ch, turn.

Inc row Miss the first st, 1 dc in next 5 dc, 2 dc in next 15 dc, 1 dc in next 4 dc, 1 dc in turning ch, 1 ch, turn (40 dc plus turning ch).

Work six rows in dc, ending last row with 5 ch, turn.

Edging

1 dc in second st, 5 ch, miss 4 dc, * (2 tr, 2 ch, 2 tr) in next dc (shell made), 5 ch, miss 4 dc, 1 dc in next dc, 5 ch; rep from *, ending with 1 dc in turning ch, 3 ch, turn.

Next row 1 dc in next space, 5 ch, * (2 tr, 2 ch, 2 tr) in 2 ch space of shell, 5 ch. 1 dc in single dc, 5 ch; rep from *; omit last 5 ch at end of row.

Skirt

Starting at back waist edge of bodice, rejoin thread with a sl st, 1 ch, work 51 dc across bodice, 1 ch, turn.

Next row Miss first st, 2 dc in next and every st to last st, 1 dc in turning ch, 3 ch, turn.

Work one row in tr, end with 3 ch, turn.

Foundation row Miss first st, (1 tr, 2 ch, 1 tr) in next st; rep from *, ending with 1 tr in turning ch, 3 ch, turn.

First pattern row * (2 tr, 1 ch, 2 tr) in 2 ch space; rep from *, ending with 1 tr in turning ch, 4 ch, turn.

Second pattern row * (1 tr, 2 ch, 1 tr) in 1 ch space; rep from *, ending with 1 tr in turning ch, 3 ch, turn.

Rep the two pattern rows for length required – approx 5–6.5cm (2 to 2½in). Fasten off.

Work a row of dc around the neck edge.

UNDERSKIRT

Make 40 ch, 1 dc in second ch from hook, 1 dc in each ch to end, 1 ch, turn.

Work one row in dc ending with 3 ch, turn.

Next row Miss first st, 2 tr in each dc to end, 1 tr in turning ch, 3 ch, turn.

Work in rows of trebles until the underskirt measures 1.5cm (½in) less than the skirt, end the last row with 1 ch, turn.

Work one row in dc, increasing 3 sts across, 5 ch, turn.

Rep the two edging rows as on the sleeve. Fasten off.

Sew up back seam of underskirt, fit on doll. Run a length of thread through waist, pull up to fit. Sew up the back seam on the skirt to within 1.5cm (½in) of the waist, fit on doll, sew up rest of seam. Run a length of thread through sleeve just above edging, pull up to fit, do the same with the waist.

HAT

Work 4 ch, join into a ring with a sl st, 1 ch, 7 dc into ring, sl st to join.

Next row 1 ch, 1 dc into same st, 2 dc in each dc, sl st to join.

Next row 3 ch, 1 dc in same st, (3 ch, 1 dc) in each st to end, 3 ch, sl st to base of first 3 ch.

Next row sl st to centre of first 3 ch loop, * 3 ch, 1 dc in next 3 ch loop; rep from *, ending with 3 ch, sl st to base of first 3 ch made.

Rep the last row four times more.

Next row sl st to centre of first 3 ch loop, 1 dc in same loop, * 6 ch, sl st into the dc just worked, 3 ch, 1 dc in next 3 ch loop; rep from *, ending the last rep with a sl st into first dc worked. Fasten off.

Glue ribbon bow and rose at the back.

3

LADIESWEAR

Ladies are always a joy to dress. In this chapter I have provided designs for the modern miss, the Victorian lady, and even a 'plus-size' lady. Over the years the fashion for wearing hats has declined. However, just in case your lady is a hat lover, each design in this chapter has a hat of some description. Berets, picture hats, bonnets – there is something here to please even the fussiest of ladies. The chapter ends with a design which is not for the faint-hearted: the blushing bride. Although not difficult to work, it is time-consuming, but the finished effect is well worth the time involved. I have also included instructions for making a very simple bouquet from quilling paper or silk roses and ribbons.

① WAISTCOAT, SKIRT AND TOP

Materials

One-ply yarn: approx.
60 metres) in main
colour (M), approx. 30
metres in contrast
colour (C)

1.25mm (US #8)
crochet hook

Tiny buttons or beads

Mini pompon

WAISTCOAT

Using M, make 38 ch, 1 dc in second ch from
hook, 1 dc in each ch to end, 1 ch, turn (37 dc
plus turning ch).

Next row Miss first st, 1 dc in each dc, end with
1 dc in turning ch, 3 ch, turn.

First pattern row Miss first st, 1 tr in each dc to
end, 1 tr in turning ch, 1 ch, turn.

Second pattern row Miss first st, 1 dc in each tr,
end with 1 dc in turning ch, 3 ch, turn. Rep the
two pattern rows twice more and the first pattern
row again.

Divide for armholes

Next row Miss first st, 1 dc in next 8 tr, 3 ch,
turn.

Next row Miss first st, 1 tr in each dc, end with
1 tr in turning ch, 1 ch, turn.

Rep last two rows twice more and the first of
these rows again. Fasten off.

Return to main piece, miss the next 2 tr, rejoin
yarn to next tr with a sl st, 1 ch, 1 dc in next 15
tr, 3 ch, turn.

Next row Miss first st, 1 tr in each dc, 1 tr in

turning ch, 1 ch, turn.

Next row Miss first st, 1 dc in each tr, end with 1 dc in turning ch, 3 ch, turn.

Rep last two rows twice. Fasten off.

Return to main piece, miss the next 2 tr, rejoin yarn to next tr with a sl st, 1 ch, dc to end, 1 dc in turning ch, 3 ch, turn.

Next row Miss first st, 1 tr in each dc, 1 tr in turning ch, 1 ch, turn.

Next row Miss first st, 1 dc in each tr, end with 1 dc in turning ch, 3 ch, turn.

Rep last two rows twice. Fasten off.

Sew up shoulder seams, leaving a gap for the neck. Starting at bottom front corner, rejoin yarn with a sl st, 1 ch, 2 dc into corner; work a row of dc working up front, across neck, down front and across bottom, working 3 dc at each corner. Fold over lapels and catch down with a few stitches. Work a row of dc around each armhole. Sew on tiny buttons or beads.

SKIRT

Using M, make 24 ch, 1 dc in second ch from hook, 1 dc in each ch to end, 1 ch, turn (23 dc plus turning ch). Work two rows in dc.

Inc row Miss first st, 3 dc in each dc, end with 1 dc in turning ch, 1 ch, turn.

Work one row in dc ending with 3 ch, turn.

First pattern row Miss first st, 1 tr in each dc to end, 1 tr in turning ch, 1 ch, turn.

Second pattern row Miss first st, 1 dc in each tr to end, 1 dc in turning ch, 3 ch, turn. Rep the last two rows six times more, ending the last row with 1 ch, turn.

Next row 1 dc in the first and second sts, * 3 ch, 1 dc in next 2 dc; rep from * to end. Fasten off.

Sew up back seam to within 2.5cm (1in) of waist edge. Fit on doll, sew up the rest of the seam, sew on tiny buttons or beads.

JUMPER

Using C, make 16 ch, 1 dc in second ch from hook, 1 dc in each ch to end, 1 ch, turn (15 dc plus turning ch). Work 12 rows in dc, ending the

last row with 14 ch, turn.

Next row 1 dc into second ch from hook, 1 dc into each ch, dc to end, 1 dc in turning ch, 14 ch, turn.

Next row 1 dc into second ch from hook, 1 dc into each ch, dc to end, 1 dc in turning ch, 1 ch, turn (43 dc plus turning ch). Work nine rows in dc.

Next row Miss first st, 1 dc in next 16 dc, 10 ch, miss next 10 dc, dc to end, 1 dc in turning ch, 1 ch, turn.

Next row Miss first st, 1 dc in next 16 dc, 1 dc in each of 10 ch, dc to end, 1 dc in turning ch, 1 ch, turn.

Work nine rows in dc.

Next row Miss first st, 1 dc in next 29 dc, 1 ch, turn.

Next row Miss first st, 1 dc in next 15 dc, 1 ch, turn.

Work 11 rows in dc. Fasten off.

Work a row of dc around neck edge.

Cuff

Rejoin yarn to sleeve edge with a sl st, 1 ch, 10 dc across cuff, 1 ch, turn.

Work two more rows in dc. Fasten off.

Sew up side and sleeve seams.

BOBBLE HAT

Using M, make 26 ch. 1 dc in second ch from hook, 1 dc in each ch to end, 1 ch, turn (25 dc plus turning ch).

Next row Miss first st, 1 dc in each dc, 1 dc in turning ch, 1 ch, turn.

Work two rows in dc.

Change to C and work another five rows in dc.

Next row Miss first st, * dc 2 tog, 1 dc; rep from *.

Work one row in dc.

Rep the last dec row once more.

Next row Work 2 dc tog across row. Fasten off, draw yarn through sts, pull up tight.

Sew up seam, turn over the first few rows for a brim, glue a mini pompon to top.

COAT AND HAT

Materials

One-ply yarn (approx. 60 metres)

1.25mm (US #8) crochet hook

Short length of gold chain

Four small gold beads for buttons

COAT

Main piece

Make 44 ch, 1 dc in second ch from hook, 1 dc in each ch to end, 1 ch, turn (43 dc plus turning ch). Work 34 rows in dc, or to length required.

Divide for armholes

Miss first st, 1 dc in next 10 dc, 1 ch, turn.
Work 10 rows in dc.
Next row Miss first st, 1 dc in next 8 dc, 1 ch, turn.
Work one row in dc. Fasten off.

Back

Return to main piece. Miss 2 dc, rejoin yarn to next dc with a sl st, 1 ch, 1 dc in next 17 dc, 1 ch, turn.
Work 12 rows in dc. Fasten off.

Second front

Return to main piece. Miss 2 dc, rejoin yarn to next dc with a sl st, 1 ch, dc to end, 1 dc in turning ch, 1 ch, turn.
Work nine rows in dc.
Next row Miss first st, 1 dc in next 8 dc, 1 ch, turn.
Work one row in dc. Fasten off.
Sew up shoulder seams for approx 1cm (⅜in).

Collar

With wrong side facing, rejoin yarn to neck edge.
Work 2 ch in first st, work 24 dc around neck edge, 1 ch, turn.
Work six rows in dc, increasing 1 st at beg of each row. Fasten off.
Work one row in dc along each front.

Sleeves (make two)

Make 22 ch, 1 dc into second ch from hook, 1 dc in each ch to end, 1 ch, turn (21 dc plus turning ch).
Work 24 rows in dc, or to length required. Fasten off.
Sew up sleeve and set into armhole. Attach a length of gold chain at the back for a false belt, and gold beads for buttons.

HAT

Make 4 ch, join into a ring with a sl st, work 9 dc into ring, sl st to join.
Next row 1 ch, 1 dc in same space, 2 dc in each dc to end, sl st to join.
Next row 1 ch, 1 dc in same space. * 1 dc in next dc, 2 dc in next dc; rep from *, ending with 1 dc, sl st to join.
Next row 1 ch, 1 dc in each dc, sl st to join.
Work 12 rows in dc. Fasten off.
Turn up three rows for brim, spray liberally with spray-on starch or use dilute white PVA glue.
Make a dip running from front to back. Dry thoroughly.

SUIT AND HAT

Materials

One 5g ball of DMC Fil à Dentelles 80 in main colour (M)

Small amount in a contrast colour (C) for the skirt, jacket and hat

Small amount in a second contrast colour (D) for the sleeveless top

0.75mm (US #12) crochet hook

Silk-ribbon roses for the hat

SLEEVELESS TOP

Using D, make 40 ch, 1 dc in second ch from hook, 1 dc in each ch to end, 1 ch, turn (39 dc plus turning ch).

Work 11 rows in dc.

Divide for armholes

Miss first st, 1 dc in next 7 dc, 1 ch, turn.

Work eight rows in dc. Fasten off.

Front

Return to main piece, miss next 3 dc, rejoin thread to next dc with a sl st, 1 ch, 1 dc in next 17 dc, 1 ch, turn.

Work 10 rows in dc. Fasten off.

Second back

Return to main piece, miss next 3 dc, rejoin thread to next dc with a sl st, 1 ch, 1 dc in each dc to end, 1 dc in turning ch, 1 ch, turn.

Work 10 rows in dc. Fasten off.

Sew up the shoulder seams for approx. 0.5cm (¼in).

Work three rows in dc around the neck edge.

Work one row in dc around each armhole.

Rejoin thread to bottom edge of jumper with a sl st, 1 ch, work 22 dc across edge, 1 ch, turn.

Work three rows in dc. Fasten off.

Fit on doll, sew up the back seam.

SKIRT

With M, make 30 ch, 1 dc in second ch from hook, 1 dc in each ch to end, 1 ch, turn (29 dc plus turning ch).

Work three rows in dc.

First inc row 1 dc in first st (first inc made), * 1 dc in next dc, 2 dc in next dc; rep from * to end, 1 dc in turning ch, 1 ch, turn (44 dc plus turning ch).

Work two rows in dc.

Second inc row Miss first dc, * 2 dc in next dc, 1 dc in next dc; rep from *, ending with the last dc in turning ch, 1 ch, turn (66 dc plus turning ch).

Work in dc for approx 5.5cm (2¼in) or length required. Fasten off.

With C, rejoin thread to waist edge, work two rows of dc down the first front, across the bottom edge, and up second front, working 3 dc at each corner. Fasten off.

JACKET

With M, make 46 ch, 1 dc in second ch from hook, 1 dc in each ch to end, 1 ch, turn (45 dc plus turning ch).

Work 15 rows in dc.

Divide for armholes

Miss first st, 1 dc in next 8 dc, 1 ch, turn.

Work nine rows in dc.

Neck shaping

* Miss first st, 1 dc in next 5 dc, 1 ch, turn.

Next row Miss first st, dc 2 tog, dc to end, 1 dc in turning ch, 1 ch, turn.

Work one row in dc.

Rep the last two rows once more. Fasten off. *

Back

Return to main piece, miss next 4 dc, rejoin thread to next dc with a sl st, 1 ch, 1 dc in next 19 dc, 1 ch, turn.

Work 14 rows in dc. Fasten off.

Second front

Return to main piece, miss next 4 dc, rejoin thread to next dc with a sl st, 1 ch, 1 dc in each dc to end, 1 dc in turning ch, 1 ch, turn.

Work eight rows in dc. Rep neck shaping from * to * as on first front. Fasten off.

Sew up the shoulder seams.

With C, work two rows in dc around neck, front edges and bottom edge, working 3 dc at each corner. Fasten off.

Sleeves (make two)

With C, make 20 ch, 1 dc in second ch from hook, 1 dc in each ch to end, 1 ch, turn (19 dc plus turning ch).

Work one row in dc.

Change to M and work 15 rows in dc.

** **Next row** 1 dc in first st (first inc made), work in dc to end, working 2 dc in last dc (second inc made), 1 dc in turning ch, 1 ch, turn (21 dc plus turning ch).

Work four rows in dc. **

Rep from ** to ** twice (25 dc plus turning ch).

Fasten off.

Sew up side seam, fit and sew into armhole.

PILLBOX HAT

With M, make 4 ch, join into a ring with a sl st. Work 8 dc into ring, sl st to join.

First row 1 ch, 1 dc into each dc, sl st to join.

Second row 1 ch, 1 dc into same st, * 2 dc into next dc; rep from *, sl st to join (17 dc).

Rep the last two rows once (35 dc).

Rep the first row 10 times.

Change to C, work the first row three times. Fasten off.

Use either watered-down white PVA glue or spray starch to stiffen; I used the top of a glue stick as a mould for the hat. When dry, add ribbon roses or other decorations.

Materials

One reel of DMC
Broder Machine
30 in white for
underwear

One 200-metre reel of
Moravia 40/2 or other
linen thread in A

Small amount in B for
dress, jacket and beret

0.60mm (US #14)
crochet hook

Pompon for beret

UNDIES

Using DMC Broder Machine 30, make 35 ch, 1
dc in second ch from hook, dc to end, 1 ch, turn.
Work two rows in dc.

Foundation row (right side) 1 dc in first st,
* 2 ch, miss next st, 1 dc in next st; rep from *,
ending with 1 dc in turning ch,
3 ch, turn.

First pattern row 1 tr in first st, * 3 tr in next dc;
rep from *, ending with 2 tr in turning ch, 1 ch,
turn.

Second pattern row 1 dc in first st, * 2 ch, 1 dc
in centre of 3 tr group; rep from *, ending with
1 dc in turning ch, 3 ch, turn.

Rep the two pattern rows to length required.

Edging

1 dc in first st, * 5 tr in next dc, 1 dc in next dc;
rep from *, ending with 1 dc in turning ch. Fasten
off.

Measure against doll, mark the crotch, sew the
front, half the back, and leg seams, fit on doll,
sew up the rest of the back seam. Run a gathering
thread through the waist, pull up to fit.

UNDERSKIRT

Using DMC Broder Machine 30, make 79 ch,
work the foundation and pattern rows as for
the knickers.

Sew up the back seam and finish off as
for the knickers.

DRESS

Bodice

With Moravia Linen (A), make 24 ch, 1 dc in
second ch from hook, dc to end, 1 ch, turn
(23 dc plus turning ch).

Work two rows in dc.

Inc row Miss first st, 1 dc in next 3 dc,
(2 dc in next dc [inc made], 1 dc in next dc) 6
times, 1 dc in last dc, 1 dc in turning ch,
1 ch, turn.

Work four rows in dc.

Armhole

Miss first st, 1 dc in next 26 dc, 1 ch, turn.

Next row Miss first st, 1 dc in next 23 dc, 1 ch,
turn.

Work eight rows in dc.

Divide for neck

Miss first st, 1 dc in next 6 dc, 1 ch, turn.

Work four rows in dc, ending the last row with 5 ch, turn.

** **Next row** 1 dc in second ch from hook, 1 dc in each ch, dc to end, 1 ch, turn.

Work eight rows in dc, ending the last row with 3 ch, turn.

Next row 1 dc in second ch from hook, 1 dc in next ch, dc to end, 1 dc in turning ch, 1 ch, turn.

Work eight rows in dc. Fasten off. **

Return to neck edge, miss the next 10 dc, rejoin thread to next dc with a sl st, 1 ch, dc to end, 1 dc in turning ch, 1 ch, turn.

Work five rows in dc, ending the last row with 5 ch, turn.

Rep from ** to **.

Armhole edging

Using B, rejoin thread to armhole edge with a sl st, 1 ch, work 23 dc across armhole, 1 ch, turn. Work two rows in dc. Fasten off.

Neck edging

As armhole, but work 27 dc.

Sew up the side seams.

Skirt

With A and with wrong side facing, rejoin thread to back waist edge with a sl st, 3 ch, work approx 100 tr across waist, 1 ch, turn.

First pattern row Miss first st, 1 dc in each tr to end, 1 dc in turning ch, 3 ch, turn.

Second pattern row Miss first st, 1 tr in each dc to end, 1 tr in turning ch, 1 ch, turn.

Rep the last two rows until the skirt measures approx the same length as the underskirt, ending after the second row.

Change to B and work three rows in dc. Fasten off.

Sew up the back skirt seam to within 2.5cm (1in) of waist, fit on doll and sew up the rest of the seam. Gather tightly around the neck edge and the waist.

JACKET

With Moravia linen A, make 68 ch, 1 dc in second ch from hook, 1 dc in each ch to end, 1 ch, turn (67 dc plus turning ch).

Work 20 rows in dc, or to length required.

Divide for armholes

Miss first st, 1 dc in next 12 dc, 1 ch, turn.

Work one row in dc.

Dec row

Miss first st, dc to the last 2 dc, dc 2 tog, 1 dc in turning ch, 1 ch, turn.

Work one row in dc.

Rep the dec row once more.

Work two rows in dc.

Next row Miss first st, 1 dc in next 4 dc, 1 ch, turn.

Work five rows in dc. Fasten off.

Return to main piece, miss the next 8 dc, rejoin thread to next dc with a sl st, 1 ch, 1 dc in next 25 dc, 1 ch, turn.

Work one row in dc.

Dec row Miss first st, dc 2 tog, dc to last 2 dc,

dc 2 tog, 1 dc in turning ch, 1 ch, turn.

Work one row in dc.

Rep the dec row once more.

Work eight rows in dc. Fasten off.

Return to main piece, miss the next 8 dc, rejoin thread to next dc with a sl st, 1 ch, 1 dc in each dc to end, 1 dc in turning ch, 1 ch, turn.

Work one row in dc.

Dec row Miss first st, dc 2 tog, dc to end, 1 dc in turning ch, 1 ch, turn.

Work one row in dc.

Rep the dec row once more.

Work three rows in dc.

Next row Miss first st, 1 dc in next 4 dc, 1 ch, turn.

Work five rows in dc. Fasten off.

Sleeves (work two)

Rejoin thread to the centre underarm with a sl st, 1 ch, work 32 dc around armhole, 1 ch, turn.

Work in dc until length required.

Change to B and work two rows in dc. Fasten off.

Sew up the sleeve seam.

Edging

Using B, and with wrong side facing, rejoin thread at one corner with a sl st, 1 ch, 2 dc in the same st. Work up the front, round the neck, down the second front and across the bottom in dc, working 3 dc at each corner, sl st to join.

1 ch, work one more row in dc, working 3 dc at each corner, sl st to join. Fasten off.

BERET

Make 4 ch, join into a ring with a sl st. 3 ch, 7 tr into ring, sl st to join.

Next row 3 ch, 1 tr in same st, 2 tr in each tr to end, sl st to join.

Rep the last row once more.

Next row 3 ch, 1 tr in each tr to end, inc 8 tr evenly all round, sl st to join.

Next row 3 ch, 1 tr in each tr, sl st to join.

Rep the last row three times more. Fasten off.

Sew in ends, glue a small pompon to top of beret.

⑪ DRESS, STOLE AND HAT

Materials

One-ply yarn (approx. 80 metres)

1.25mm (US #8) crochet hook

Silk ribbon and ribbon roses, feathers, etc.

DRESS

Bodice

Make 14 ch, 1 dc in second ch from hook, 1 dc in each ch to end, 1 ch, turn.

Work 11 rows in dc.

Next row Miss first st, 1 dc in next 3 dc, 1 ch, turn.

Next row Miss first st, 1 dc in next 2 dc, 1 dc in turning ch, 1 ch, turn.

Work six more rows in dc. Fasten off.

Return to main part. Miss next 6 dc, rejoin yarn to next dc with a sl st, 1 ch, 1 dc in next 2 dc, 1 dc in turning ch.

Work seven rows in dc, working 6 ch at the end of the last row, work across the first piece in dc, 1 dc in turning ch, 1 ch, turn.

Next row Miss first st, 1 dc in each dc, 1 dc in each ch, 1 dc in each dc to end, 1 dc in turning ch, 1 ch, turn.

Work 10 rows in dc. Fasten off.

Sew up side seams for 1.5cm (⅝in).

Skirt

Starting at centre back, rejoin yarn with a sl st, 1 ch, 2 dc in each stitch all round, end with 1 dc in last st (53 dc plus ch), 3 ch, turn.

Foundation row (1 tr, 2 ch, 1 tr) in same dc, * miss 2 dc (1 tr, 2 ch, 1 tr) in next dc; rep from * to end of row, 3 ch, turn.

First pattern row * 4 tr in 2 ch space; rep from *
to end of row, ending with 1 tr in last st, 4 ch,
turn.

Second pattern row * (1 tr, 2 ch, 1 tr) in centre
4 tr group; rep from *, ending with 1 tr in turning
ch, 3 ch, turn.

Rep last two rows five times more, then first row
once more. Fasten off.

Sew up back skirt seam. Thread ribbon through
waist and tie in a bow.

STOLE

Make 65 ch.

Foundation row 1 tr
in sixth ch from hook, 2 ch,
1 tr in same ch, * miss 2 ch,
(1 tr, 2 ch, 1 tr) in next ch;
rep from * to end of ch, 3 ch, turn.
Rep the two pattern rows as on the
skirt until stole is required depth, ending
with the first pattern row. Fasten off.

HAT

Make 4 ch, join into a ring with a sl st, 1 ch, 9 dc
into ring, sl st to join.

Next row 1 ch, 1 dc in same st, 2 dc in each st to
end, sl st to join (19 dc plus ch).

Next row 1 ch, 1 dc in same st * 1 dc in next st,
2 dc in next st; rep from *, ending with 1 dc, sl
st to join (29 dc plus ch).

Next row 1 ch, 1 dc in each dc, sl st to
join.

Work seven more rows in dc.

Next row 1 ch, 1 dc in same st,
* 1 dc in next dc, 2 dc in next dc;
rep from *, sl st to join.

Next row 1 ch, miss first dc,
1 dc in each dc to end, sl st to
join.

Rep last two rows twice more.

Edging

3 ch, * miss first dc, 1 tr in next
dc, 1 tr in missed dc; rep from *; end with a sl st
into top of 3 ch. Fasten off.

Stiffen with spray starch or dilute PVA glue, turn
up brim at one side, leave to dry thoroughly. Trim
with silk ribbon, roses or feathers as required.

DRESS, PANTALOONS AND HAT

Materials

One reel of Madeira
Tanne/Cotona 30

0.60mm (US #14)
crochet hook

Silk ribbon, roses,
feathers, etc.

PANTALOONS (make two pieces)

Make 20 ch, 1 dc in second ch from hook, 1 dc in each ch, 1 ch, turn.

Work two rows in dc, working 3 ch at the end of the last row, turn.

Inc row Miss first st, 2 tr in each dc to end, 1 tr in turning ch, 3 ch, turn.

Work in tr for length required.

Edging

First pattern row Miss first st, 1 tr in next tr, * 2 ch, miss 1 tr, 1 tr in next tr; rep from *, ending with 2 ch, miss 1 tr, 1 tr in turning ch, 4 ch, turn.

Second pattern row * 1 dtr, 3 ch, 1 dtr, in each 2 ch space, end with 1 dtr in turning ch. Fasten off. Make a second leg. Measure against doll, mark the crotch, sew up the leg, front and half the back seam, fit on doll, sew up rest of seam. Run a gathering thread through waist, pull up to fit.

DRESS

Bodice

Make 17 ch, 1 dc in second ch from hook, 1 dc in each ch to end, 1 ch, turn (16 dc plus turning ch).

Work nine rows in dc.

Inc row Miss first st, 2 dc in each dc to end, 1 dc in turning ch, 1 ch, turn (31 dc plus turning ch).

Work two rows in dc.

Armhole shaping

Miss first st, 1 dc in next 28 dc, 1 ch, turn.

Next row Miss first st, 1 dc in next 25 dc, 1 ch, turn.

Work one row in dc.

Divide for neck

Miss first st, 1 dc in next 3 dc, 1 ch, turn.

Work 17 rows in dc, ending the last row with 3 ch, turn (armhole edge).

* **Next row** 1 dc in second ch from hook, 1 dc in next ch, dc to end, 3 ch, turn (back edge).

Next row 1 dc in second ch from hook, 1 dc in

next ch, dc to end, 1 dc in turning ch, 1 ch, turn.

Work 11 rows in dc on these 9 dc and turning ch. Fasten off. *

Return to front neck, miss the next 18 dc, rejoin thread to next dc with a sl sl, 1 ch, dc to end, 1 ch, turn (3 dc plus turning ch).

Work 16 rows in dc, ending the last row with 3 ch, turn (armhole edge). Rep from * to *.

Sleeves (make two)

Rejoin thread at armhole edge with a sl st, work 38 dc across, 4 ch, turn.

Foundation row Miss first st, 1 tr in next dc, * miss 2 dc, (1 tr, 3 ch, 1 tr) in next dc; rep from *, ending with (1 tr, 3 ch, 1 tr) in last dc, 1 tr in turning ch, 4 ch, turn.

Pattern row * (1 tr, 1 ch, 1 tr) in 3 ch space; rep from * to end, 1 tr in turning ch, 4 ch, turn.

Rep the pattern row four times, ending last row with 1 ch, turn.

Dec row * 1 dc in 3 ch space, 1 dc in tr; rep from *, ending with 1 dc in turning ch, 1 ch, turn.

Work two rows in dc. Fasten off.

Sew up side and sleeve seams.

Underskirt

Rejoin thread at back waist edge with a sl st, 3 ch, 1 tr in same st, work 70 more tr across front and both backs, 3 ch, turn.

Next row Miss first st, 2 tr in each tr to end, 1 tr in turning ch, 1 ch, turn.

Foundation row Miss first st, 1 tr in next tr, * 2 ch, miss 1 tr, 1 tr in next tr; rep from *, ending with 2 ch, miss 1 tr, 1 tr in turning ch, 4 ch, turn.

Pattern row * 1 tr in 2 ch space, 2 ch; rep from *, ending with 1 tr in turning ch, 4 ch, turn.

Rep the pattern row until length required.

Edging

* 1 dtr, 3 ch, 1 dtr in each 2 ch space, end with 1 dtr in turning ch. Fasten off.

Sew up skirt seam to within 2.5cm (1in) of waist, fit on doll, sew up rest of skirt and bodice seam. Run a gathering thread through the sleeve edge, pull up to fit.

Overskirt

Make 176 ch, 1 dc in second ch from hook, 1 dc in each ch, 1 ch, turn.

Work one row in dc, 1 ch, turn.

Foundation row Miss first st, 1 dc in next dc, * miss 2 dc, (1 tr, [1 ch, 1 tr] 4 times) in next dc, miss 2 dc, 1 dc in next dc; rep from * to end, 5 ch, turn.

First pattern row * 1 dc in second 1 ch space, 1 ch, 1 dc in third 1 ch space, 2 ch, 1 tr in dc, 2 ch; rep from *, ending with 1 tr in turning ch, 1 ch, turn.

Second pattern row 1 dc in first st, (1 tr, [1 ch, 1 tr] 4 times) in 1 ch space, 1 dc in tr; rep from *, ending with 1 dc in turning ch, 5 ch, turn.

Rep the two pattern rows for length required, ending with the second pattern row. Fasten off. Sew up the back seam, run a gathering thread through waist edge, fit on doll, pull up to fit. Slipstitch to the bodice.

HAT

Make 4 ch, sl st to join into a ring. 3 ch, work 11 tr into ring, sl st to join.

First inc row 3 ch, 1 tr in same st, 2 tr in each tr

to end, sl st to join (23 tr plus ch).

Second inc row 3 ch, 1 tr in same st, 1 tr in next tr, * 2 tr in next tr, 1 tr in next tr; rep from * to end, sl st to join (35 tr plus ch).

Next row 1 ch, 1 dc in each tr, sl st to join. Work nine rows in dc.

Third inc row 3 ch, 1 tr in same st, 2 tr in each dc to end, sl st to join.

Next row 3 ch, 1 tr in each tr to end, sl st to join.

Fourth inc row 3 ch, 1 tr in next tr, * 2 tr in next tr, 1 tr in next tr; rep from *, sl st to join. 4 ch.

Edging

Miss first st, 1 dc in next dc, * miss 2 dc, (1 tr, [1 ch, 1 tr] 4 times) in next dc, miss 2 dc, 1 dc in next dc; rep from * to end. Fasten off.

Stiffen with spray starch or dilute PVA glue. Decorate with ribbon roses, feathers, etc.

DRESS, BONNET AND UNDIES EDGING

DRESS

Bodice

Make 17 ch, 1 dc in second ch from hook, 1 dc in each ch to end, 1 ch, turn (16 dc plus turning ch). Work nine rows in dc.

Inc row Miss first st, 2 dc in each dc to end, 1 dc in turning ch, 1 ch, turn (31 dc plus turning ch). Work two rows in dc.

Armhole shaping

Miss first st, 1 dc in next 28 dc, 1 ch, turn.

Next row Miss first st, 1 dc in next 25 dc, 1 ch, turn.

Work one row in dc.

Divide for neck

Miss first st, 1 dc in next 3 dc, 1 ch, turn.

Work 17 rows in dc, ending the last row with 3 ch, turn (armhole edge).

* **Next row** 1 dc in second ch from hook, 1 dc in next ch, dc to end, 3 ch, turn (back edge).

Next row 1 dc in second ch from hook, 1 dc in next ch, dc to end, 1 dc in turning ch, 1 ch, turn.

Work 11 rows in dc (9 dc plus turning ch). Fasten off. *

Return to front neck, miss the next 18 dc, rejoin thread to next dc with a sl st, 1 ch, dc to end, 1 ch, turn (3 dc plus turning ch).

Work 16 rows in dc, ending the last row with 3 ch, turn (armhole edge). Rep from * to *.

Skirt

Rejoin thread at the back waist edge with a sl st, 3 ch, work 77 tr across front and both backs, 3 ch, turn.

Foundation row 1 tr in first st, * 3 ch, miss 2 sts, 1 dc in next st, 3 ch, 3 tr in same st, miss 2 sts, (1 tr, 1 ch, 1 tr) in next st; rep from *, ending last rep with 2 tr in turning ch instead of (1 tr, 1 ch, 1 tr), 3 ch, turn.

Pattern row A 1 tr in first st, * 3 ch, 1 dc in top of 3 ch, 3 ch, 3 tr in same 3 ch space, miss next 3 ch space, (1 tr, 1 ch, 1 tr) in 1 ch, space; rep from *, ending last rep with 2 tr in turning ch instead of (1 tr, 1 ch, 1 tr), 3 ch, turn.

Materials

One reel of Madeira Tanne/Cotona 30

0.60mm (US #14) crochet hook

Ribbon, flowers, feathers, etc.

Pattern row B 1 tr in first st, (1 tr, 1 ch, 1 tr) in 1 ch space, * 3 ch, 1 dc in top of 3 ch, 3 ch, 3 tr in same 3 ch space, (1 tr, 1 ch. 1 tr) in next 1 ch space; rep from *, ending with (1 tr, 1 ch, 1 tr) in 1 ch space, 2 tr in turning ch, 3 ch, turn.
Rep the last row 16 times or until length required. Fasten off.

Collar

Rejoin thread at back neck with a sl st, 3 ch, work 66 dc all round neck edge.
Work the foundation row as on skirt.
Work in pattern row A for five rows. Fasten off.
Sew up the back skirt seam to within 2.5 cm (1in) of the waist, fit on doll, sew up rest of seam.

UNDIES

I used silk to make the underskirt and a pair of pantaloons. For the pantaloons cut two rectangles of silk to suit size of doll. Sew up the back and front seam to the crotch, then the leg seams. For the underskirt, cut a rectangular piece of silk, sew up the back seam. After sewing on the edgings, fit on doll, run a gathering thread through waist edges, pull up to fit.

Edging

Make 6 ch.
Foundation row (1 tr, 2 ch, 1 tr, 2 ch, 1 tr) into the sixth ch from the hook, 5 ch, turn.
Pattern row (1 tr, 2 ch, 1 tr, 2 ch, 1 tr) in centre tr of the previous row, 5 ch, turn.
Rep the pattern row for length required, do not turn at end of last row.

Heading

* 1 dc in next 5 ch loop, 5 ch; rep from *, ending with 1 tr in first st. Fasten off and sew to the undies.

BONNET

4 ch, join into a ring with a sl st, 3 ch, work 11 tr into ring, sl st to join.
First inc row 3 ch, 1 tr in same st, 2 tr in each tr, sl st to join (23 tr plus turning ch).

Rep the pattern row 10 times more.
Inc row 1 tr in first st, * 3 ch, 1 dc in top of 3 ch, 3 ch, 3 tr in same 3 ch space, (1 tr, 1 ch, 1 tr) in next 3 ch space, (1 tr, 1 ch, 1 tr) in next 1 ch space; rep from *, ending last rep with 2 tr in turning ch, 3 ch, turn.
Next row 1 tr in first st, (1 tr, 1 ch, 1 tr) in 1 ch space, * 3 ch, 1 dc in top of 3 ch, 3 ch, 3 tr in same 3 ch space, (1 tr, 1 ch, 1 tr) in next 3 ch space, 3 ch, (1 dc, 3 ch, 3 tr) in next 1 ch space, (1 tr, 1 ch, 1 tr) in next 1 ch space; rep from *, ending with 3 ch, 3 tr in same 3 ch space, (1 tr, 1 ch, 1 tr) in next 3 ch space, 2 tr in turning ch, 3 ch, turn.

Second inc row 3 ch, 1 tr in same st, 1 tr in next tr, * 2 tr in next tr, 1 tr in next tr; rep from *, sl st to join (35 tr plus turning ch).

Next row 1 ch, work 1 dc in each tr, 1 ch, turn.

Work 12 rows in dc, ending the last row with 3 ch.

Inc row Miss first st, 2 tr in each dc to end, 1 tr in turning ch, 3 ch, turn.

Work foundation row as on skirt.

Work pattern row A three times. Fasten off.

Add ribbon ties and decorate with ribbon roses, feathers, etc.

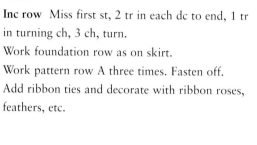

WEDDING OUTFIT

DRESS

Bodice

Make 17 ch, 1 dc in second ch from hook, 1 dc in each ch to end, 1 ch, turn (16 dc plus turning ch). Work nine rows in dc.

Inc row Miss first st, 2 dc in each dc to end, 1 dc in turning ch, 1 ch, turn (31 dc plus turning ch). Work two more rows in dc.

Armhole shaping

Miss first st, 1 dc in next 28 dc, 1 ch, turn.

Next row Miss first st, 1 dc in next 25 dc, 1 ch, turn.

Work one more row in dc.

Divide for neck

Miss first st, 1 dc in next 3 dc, 1 ch, turn.

Work 17 rows in dc, ending the last row with 3 ch, turn (armhole edge).

* **Next row** 1 dc in second ch from hook, 1 dc in next ch, dc to end, 3 ch, turn (back edge).

Next row 1 dc in second ch from hook, 1 dc in next ch, dc to end, 1 dc in turning ch, 1 ch, turn. Work 11 rows in dc (9 dc plus turning ch). Fasten off. *

Return to front neck, miss the next 18 dc, rejoin thread to next dc with a sl st, 1 ch, dc to end, 1 ch, turn (3 dc plus turning ch).

Work 16 rows in dc, ending the last row with

3 ch, turn (armhole edge).

Rep from * to *.

Sleeves (make two)

With wrong side facing, rejoin thread to armhole edge with a sl st, 1 ch, work 26 dc across armhole edge, 1 ch, turn.

Work 30 rows in dc, or length required.

Edging

First row Miss first st, 1 dc in next 3 sts, * 3 ch, miss next st, (2 tr, 2 ch, 2 tr) in next st, 3 ch, miss next st, 1 dc in next 5 sts; rep from *, ending last rep with 1 dc in last 3 sts, 1 dc in turning ch, 1 ch, turn.

Second row Miss first st, 1 dc in next st, 4 ch, * (2 tr, 2 ch, 2 tr) in 2 ch space, 4 ch, 1 dc in centre of 5 dc group, 4 ch; rep from * once more, (2 tr, 2 ch, 2 tr) in 2 ch, space, 4 ch, 1 dc in last dc, 1 dc in turning ch. Fasten off.

Sew up sleeve and side seam.

Neck edge

Rejoin thread at back neck edge with a sl st, 1 ch, work 49 dc around neck, 1 ch, turn. Work one more row in dc, decreasing 7 dc evenly across row. Fasten off.

Underskirt

Rejoin thread to back waist edge with a sl st, 3 ch, 1 tr in same st, 2 tr in each st across waist, ending with 1 tr in last st, 3 ch, turn (72 tr plus turning ch).

Work one more row in trebles.

Rep last two rows once more (144 tr plus turning ch).

First pattern row Miss 2 sts, * (1 tr, 1 ch, 1 tr) in next tr, miss 1 tr, 1 tr in next tr, miss 1 tr; rep from *, ending with 1 tr in turning ch, 3 ch, turn.

Second pattern row 1 tr in first st, * 1 tr in 1 ch, space, (1 tr, 1 ch, 1 tr) in single tr; rep from *, ending with 2 tr in turning ch, 3 ch, turn.

Third and fourth pattern rows 1 tr in each st to end, 1 tr in turning ch, 3 ch, turn.

Rep these four pattern rows for length required, ending with the third pattern row and increasing 2 sts on the last row.

Rep the two edging rows as on sleeves. Fasten off.

Sew up back seam on underskirt to within 1.25cm (½in) of waist. Fit on doll, sew up rest of back seam on underskirt and bodice. Run a gathering thread through waist and pull up to fit. Run a gathering thread through sleeves just above edging, pull up to fit.

Overskirt

Make 202 ch, 1 dc in second ch from hook, 1 dc in each ch to end, 4 ch, turn.

Foundation row 1 tr in first st, * miss 3 sts, ([1 tr, 1 ch] 3 times, 1 tr) in next st (shell made); rep from *, ending with (1 tr, 1 ch, 1 tr) in last st, 4 ch, turn.

Pattern row 1 tr in first 1 ch space, * ([1 tr, 1 ch] 3 times, 1 tr) in centre ch of shell; rep from *, ending with (1 tr, 1 ch, 1 tr) in last 1 ch space, 4 ch, turn.

Rep the last pattern row for length required. Fasten off.

Sew up back seam. Run a gathering thread through waist edge, place over the underskirt, pull up to fit. Adjust gathers evenly, slipstitch to bodice.

HEADDRESS

Make 62 ch, 1 dc in second ch from hook, 1 dc in each ch to end, 4 ch, turn.

Foundation row 1 tr in first st, * miss 1 dc, (1 tr, 1 ch, 1 tr) in next dc; rep from * to end, 4 ch, turn.

Pattern row 1 tr in first ch space, * (1 tr, 1 ch, 1 tr) in next 1 ch space; rep from * to end, 4 ch, turn.

Rep the last row 19 times more.

Inc row 1 tr in first ch space, * ([1 tr, 1 ch] 3 times, 1 tr) in next 1 ch space, (1 tr, 1 ch, 1 tr) in next 1 ch space; rep from *, ending with (1 tr, 1 ch, 1 tr) in last ch space, 4 ch, turn.

Pattern row 1 tr in first 1 ch space, * ([1 tr, 1 ch] 3 times, 1 tr) in centre ch of shell, (1 tr, 1 ch, 1 tr) in next 1 ch space; rep from * to end, 4 ch, turn.

Rep the last pattern row 14 times more.

Inc row 1 tr in first 1 ch space, * ([1 tr, 1 ch] 3 times, 1 tr) in centre of next shell, ([1 tr, 1 ch] 3 times, 1 tr) in next 1 ch space; rep from *, ending with (1 tr, 1 ch, 1 tr) in last ch space, 4 ch, turn.

Pattern row 1 tr in first 1 ch space, * ([1 tr, 1 ch] 3 times, 1 tr) in centre of next shell; rep from *,

ending with (1 tr, 1 ch, 1 tr) in last ch space. Rep pattern row 14 times more.

Inc row 1 tr in first ch space, * ([1 tr, 1 ch] 3 times, 1 tr) in centre of next shell, (1 tr, 1 ch, 1 tr) in space between shells; rep from *, ending with ([1 tr, 1 ch] 3 times, 1 tr) in centre of last shell, (1 tr, 1 ch, 1 tr) in last ch space, 4 ch, turn.

Pattern row 1 tr in first ch space, * ([1 tr, 1 ch] 3 times, 1 tr) in next shell, (1 tr, 1 ch, 1 tr) in next 1 ch space; rep from * to end, 4 ch, turn.

Rep the last row 14 times more.

Inc row 1 tr in first ch space, * ([1 tr, 1 ch] 3 times, 1 tr) in next shell, ([1 tr, 1 ch] 3 times, 1 tr) in next 1 ch space; rep from *, ending with (1 tr, 1 ch, 1 tr) in last ch space, 4 ch, turn.

Pattern row 1 tr in first ch space, * ([1 tr, 1 ch] 3 times, 1 tr) in next shell; rep from *, ending with (1 tr, 1 ch, 1 tr) in last ch space, 4 ch, turn. Rep the last row once more, omitting the 4 ch, turn at end of row, break thread. Run a gathering thread through the stitches at top of headdress, pull up tightly and fasten off. Glue the headdress to doll's head, glue comb and ribbon roses to the headdress.

GARTER (if required)

With white, make 34 ch, 1 dc in second ch from hook, 1 dc in each ch to end, 1 ch, turn.

Next row 1 tr in first st, 2 tr in each dc, end with 1 tr in turning ch.

** Change to blue, 2 ch, * (1 dc, 1 ch) in each tr to end, 1 dc in turning ch, break thread. **

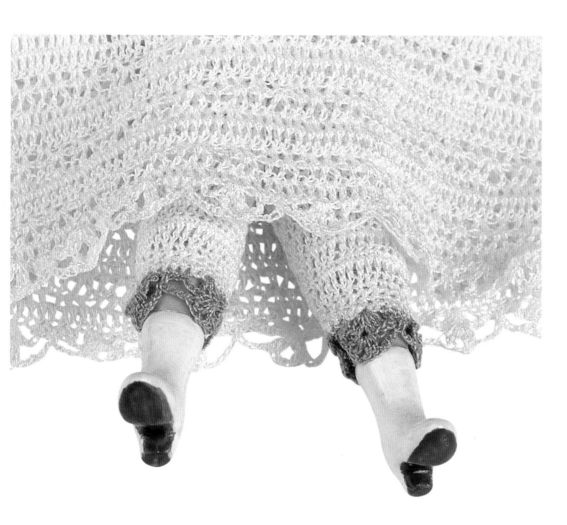

Return to ch edge of work, rejoin thread with a sl st to first ch, 3 ch, 1 tr in same st, 2 tr in each ch, end with 1 tr in last ch.

Rep from ** to **.

Sew up seam. Run a length of thread through centre of garter, fit on doll and pull up to fit, glue on a silk ribbon.

PANTALOONS (make two pieces)

Starting at the waist edge, make 17 ch 1 dc in second ch from hook, 1 dc in each ch, 1 ch, turn (16 dc plus turning ch).

Work two rows in dc, working 3 ch at end of second row.

Inc row Miss first st, * 2 tr in next dc; rep from

*, ending with 1 tr in turning ch, 1 ch, turn (31 dc plus turning ch).

Next row Work in dc, ending with 3 ch, turn.

Next row Work in tr, ending with 1 ch, turn.

Rep the last two rows 11 times.

Dec row Miss first st, * dc 2 tog, 1 dc in next st; rep from *, 1 dc in turning ch, 1 ch, turn (21 dc plus turning ch).

Work three rows in dc, inc 5 sts on the last row, 1 ch, turn (26 dc plus turning ch).

Change to blue, work the two edging rows as on the dress sleeve. Fasten off.

Measure against doll, place marker at the crotch. Sew up front and leg seams, and half the back seam. Fit on doll, sew up rest of back seam. Run a gathering thread through waist, pull up to fit.

BOUQUET

Cut the piece of card to the shape you require for the bouquet. Make two tiny holes 1cm (⅜in) apart approximately one third of the way down the card shape. Thread thin wire through the holes, twist together at the back.

Liberally cover the card with glue, placing the roses and loops where required. I made my roses from quilling paper in pink, white and lavender, with loops of green quilling paper. Silk roses and ribbon loops would look equally attractive, or any other bought flowers and foliage. Once the glue is dry, attach the bouquet to your bride by twisting the wire around her wrist.

Materials

Thin card

Strips of quilling paper

Narrow silk ribbon, or ready-made flowers

4cm (1½in) thin wire

White PVA glue

4

MENSWEAR

Most of the designs in this chapter are very simple to make; most are suited to twentieth-century man. Having created a design for a larger lady, it seemed a good idea to do likewise for the male of the species. I discovered while creating some of these designs that the same hat pattern can be moulded in different ways after stiffening to create differing styles, as in the Coat and Hat, or the Suit and Hat patterns. No bride would be complete without her groom; this gentleman sports a top hat, tails, trousers, shirt, waistcoat and cravat. This design would also be suitable for a Victorian gentleman.

TROUSERS

Materials

One-ply yarn (approx. 40 metres)

1.25mm (US #8) crochet hook

Make two pieces

Make 16 ch, 1 dc in second ch from hook, 1 dc in each ch to end, 1 ch, turn (15 dc plus turning ch).

Next row Miss first st, 1 dc in each dc, 1 dc in turning ch, 1 ch, turn.

Inc row 1 dc in first st (inc made), * 1 dc in next dc, 2 dc in next dc (inc made); rep from *, ending with 1 dc in turning ch, 1 ch, turn (23 dc plus turning ch).

Work one row in dc, ending with 2 ch, turn.

First pattern row Miss first st, 1 htr in each dc ending with 1 htr in turning ch, 1 ch, turn.

Second pattern row Miss first st, 1 dc in each htr ending with 1 dc in turning ch, 2 ch, turn.

Rep the first and second pattern rows four times.

Shape crotch

Next row 1 htr in first st (inc made), 1 htr in next 21 dc, 2 htr in next dc (inc made), 1 htr in turning ch, 1 ch, turn (25 htr plus turning ch). Work the second pattern row.

Now rep the first and second pattern rows 11 times more and the first pattern row again (or to length required). Fasten off.

Sew up the front and half the back seam, sew up the leg seams. Fit on doll, sew up rest of back seam. Run a gathering thread through waist, pull up to fit.

① LONG-SLEEVED ROUND-NECK JUMPER

Make 20 ch, 1 dc in second ch from hook, 1 dc in each ch to end, 1 ch, turn.

Work two rows in dc, increasing 3 sts on the second row, 2 ch, turn (work twice into the same stitch to increase a stitch) (22 dc plus turning ch).

First pattern row (wrong side) Miss first st, 1 htr in each dc to end, 1 htr in turning ch, 1 ch, turn.

Second pattern row Miss first st, 1 dc in each htr, 1 dc in turning ch, 2 ch, turn.

Rep the last two rows nine times, or to length required.

Next row Miss first st, 1 dc in next 5 dc, work 11 ch, miss 11 dc, dc to end, 1 dc in turning ch, 1 ch, turn.

Next row Miss first st, 1 dc in next 5 dc, 1 dc in each ch, dc to end, 1 dc in turning ch, 2 ch, turn.

Rep first and second pattern rows 10 times, decreasing 3 sts evenly on the last row (dc 2 tog to decrease a stitch).

Work two rows in dc. Fasten off.

Sleeves (both alike)

With right side facing, rejoin yarn to the 12th row from the bottom edge with a sl st, 1 ch, work 28 dc across the side, ending on the 12th row from the opposite edge.

Rep first and second pattern rows six times more, decreasing 1 st at each end of the fourth and every following fourth row.

Work the first pattern row once more (22 sts plus turning ch).

Next row Miss first st, dc 2 tog across row, 1 ch, turn (11 dc plus turning ch).

Work four rows in dc. Fasten off.

Work a row of dc around neck edge.

Sew up side seams and halfway along the sleeve seam, fit on doll, sew up the rest of the sleeve seam.

NB there are two distinct sides to this pattern; the wrong side has the more defined ridges.

Materials

One-ply yarn (approx. 40 metres)

1.25mm (US #8) crochet hook

⑪ SLEEVELESS V-NECK JUMPER

Materials

One-ply yarn (approx. 30 metres)

1.25mm (US #8) crochet hook

Make 22 ch, 1 dc in second ch from hook, 1 dc in each ch to end, 1 ch, turn (21 dc plus turning ch). Work 15 rows in dc.

Next row Miss first st, 1 dc in next 18 dc, 1 ch, turn.

Next row Miss first st, 1 dc in next 15 dc, 1 ch, turn.

Work 12 rows in dc.

Next row Miss first st, 1 dc in next 3 dc, 1 ch, turn.

Work four rows in dc.

Inc row 1 dc in first st (inc made), 1 dc in each dc, 1 dc in turning ch, 1 ch, turn.

Work one row in dc.

Rep the last two rows three times more (7 dc plus turning ch). Fasten off.

Return to neck edge, miss 8 dc, rejoin yarn to next dc with a sl st, 1 ch, dc to end, 1 dc in turning ch, 1 ch, turn.

Work five rows in dc.

Inc row 1 dc in first st (inc made), 1 dc in each dc, 1 dc in turning ch, 1 ch, turn.

Work one row in dc.

Rep the last two rows twice more, and the inc row once more (7 dc plus turning ch).

Next row Miss first st, 1 dc in each st across both fronts (15 dc plus turning ch). Work one row in dc, ending with 4 ch, turn.

Next row 1 dc in second ch from hook, 1 dc in next 2 ch, dc to end, 1 dc in turning ch, 4 ch, turn.

Rep the last row once, ending with 1 ch, turn (21 dc plus turning ch).

Work 16 rows in dc. Fasten off.

Work a row of dc around neck and armholes. Sew up the side seams.

① LONG-SLEEVED V-NECK JUMPER

Materials

One-ply yarn (approx. 40 metres)

1.25mm (US #8) crochet hook

Make 22 ch, 1 dc in second ch from hook, 1 dc in each ch to end, 1 ch, turn.

Work 20 rows in dc, 17 ch, turn.

Next row 1 dc into second ch from hook, 1 dc into each ch, dc to end, 17 ch, turn.

Next row 1 dc into second ch from hook, 1 dc into each ch, dc to end, 1 ch, turn.

Work nine rows in dc.

Next row Miss first st, 1 dc in next 23 dc, 1 ch, turn.

Work three rows in dc.

** **Inc row** Miss first st, 1 dc in each dc, ending with 2 dc in last dc, 1 dc in turning ch, 1 ch, turn.

Work one row in dc.

Repeat these last two rows until there are 27 dc plus turning ch.

Work one row in dc. Fasten off. **

Return to neck edge, miss next 8 dc, rejoin yarn to next dc with a sl st, dc to end, 1 dc in turning ch, 1 ch, turn.

Work two rows in dc. Rep from ** to **.

With right front facing, miss the first 17 dc, rejoin yarn to next dc with a sl st, 1 dc in next 10 dc, dc 11 from second front, 1 ch, turn.

Work 21 rows in dc. Fasten off.

Cuffs

Rejoin yarn to end of sleeve with a sl st, 1 ch, 12 dc across sleeve edge, 1 ch, turn.

Work two rows in dc. Fasten off.

Sew up side and sleeve seams.

Work a row of dc around neck edge, starting at centre front.

COAT AND HAT

Materials

One-ply yarn (approx. 100 metres)

1.25mm (US #8) crochet hook

Mini buttons or beads

Buckle (see List of Suppliers, page 114)

COAT

Back and front

Make 30 ch, 1 dc in second ch from hook, 1 dc in each ch to end, 1 ch, turn (29 dc plus turning ch).

Work 14 rows in dc, break yarn.

Work a second piece, working 15 rows; do not break yarn, work across the first piece (59 dc plus turning ch).

Work 30 rows in dc.

Divide for armholes

Miss first st, 1 dc in next 11 dc, 1 ch, turn.

Work 10 rows in dc.

** Neck shaping

Miss first st, 1 dc in next 5 dc, 1 ch, turn.

Work three rows in dc. Fasten off. **

Return to main piece, miss the next 6 dc, rejoin yarn with a sl st to the next dc, 1 ch, 1 dc in next 23 dc, 1 ch, turn.

Work 14 rows in dc, decreasing 4 sts evenly across the first row. Fasten off.

Return to main piece, miss the next 6 dc, rejoin yarn with a sl st to the next dc, 1 ch, dc to end, 1 dc in turning ch, 1 ch, turn.

Work 11 rows in dc.

Rep from ** to ** Sew up the shoulder seams.

Collar

Starting at the neck edge, miss the first 3 sts, rejoin yarn to the next st with a sl st, 1 ch, work 28 dc across the neck edge, ending 3 sts from the second front edge, 1 ch, turn.

Work seven rows in dc, inc 1 st at each end of the second, fourth, and sixth rows. Fasten off.

Front edge

Starting with the right side facing, work two rows of dc on both fronts.

Sleeves (make two)

Make 26 ch, 1 dc in second ch from hook, 1 dc in each ch to end, 1 ch, turn (25 dc plus turning ch).

Work 28 rows in dc, inc 1 st at each end of the 6th, 11th and 16th rows.

Adjust length of sleeve to suit doll. Fasten off.

Sew up the sleeve seams, set sleeve into the armhole, sew on mini buttons or beads.

Belt

Make 58 ch, 1 dc in second ch from hook, 1 dc in each ch to end, 1 ch, turn (57 dc plus turning ch).

Work one row in dc. Fasten off.

Attach buckle to belt. A couple of stitches at the back will secure it to the coat – or make tiny loops at each side and thread belt through.

HAT

Make 4 ch, join into a ring with a sl st.

Next row 1 ch, work 7 dc into ring, sl st to join.

Next row 1 ch, 1 dc into same st, 2 dc into each dc to end, sl st to join (15 dc).

Next row 1 ch, 1 dc into same st, * 1 dc in next dc, 2 dc in next dc; rep from *, ending with 1 dc in next st, sl st to join (23 dc).

Next row 1 ch, 1 dc into same st, * 1 dc in next 4 dc, 2 dc in next dc; rep from * 3 times more, dc to end, sl st to join.

Next row 1 ch, 1 dc in each dc, sl st to join.

Work seven rows in dc.

Next row 1 ch, 1 dc in same st, 2 dc in each dc to end, sl st to join.

Work one row in dc. Fasten off. Sew in all ends. Stiffen with commercial stiffener, thinned white PVA glue or spray starch. Shape as required and leave to dry.

SUIT

One-ply yarn in main colour M (approx 150 metres) and contrast colour C (approx 50 metres)

1.25 and 1.00mm (US #8 and #10) crochet hooks

Small buttons or beads

SHIRT

Using colour C and 1.00mm (#10) hook, make 16 ch, 1 dc in second ch from hook, 1 ch, turn (15 dc plus turning ch).

Next row Miss first st, 1 dc in each dc, 1 dc in turning ch, 2 ch, turn.

Next row Miss first st, 1 htr in next st, 1 htr in each st to end, 1 htr in turning ch, 2 ch, turn. Work in htr for 14 rows.

Next row Miss first st, 1 htr in next 4 htr, work 6 ch, miss next 5 htr, 1 htr in each htr, 1 htr in turning ch, 2 ch, turn.

Next row Miss first st, 1 htr in next 4 htr, 1 htr in each ch, 1 htr in each htr, 1 htr in turning ch, 2 ch, turn.

Work 15 rows in htr, ending the last row with 1 ch.

Now work two rows in dc. Fasten off.

Sleeves (both alike)

Rejoin yarn to the eighth htr row with a sl st, 2 ch, 18 htr ending on the eighth htr row from the opposite side, 2 ch, turn.

Work 14 rows in htr, ending with 1 ch on last row.

Next row Work in dc, decreasing 7 sts evenly across row, 1 ch, turn.

Work three rows in dc for the cuff.

Collar

Starting at centre front of neck, rejoin yarn with a sl st, 1 ch, 17 dc round neck, 1 ch, turn.

First row Miss first st, 1 dc to end, 1 dc in turning ch, 1 ch, turn.

Second row As first row, inc 5 sts evenly across the row.

Work three rows in dc. Fasten off.

Sew up side and sleeve seams.

TIE

Using M and 1.00mm (#10) hook, make 4 ch, 1 dc in second ch from hook, 1 dc in each ch, 1 ch, turn.

Next row Miss first st, 1 dc in each dc, 1 dc in turning ch, 1 ch, turn.

Rep the last row until work measures 4cm (1½in). Fasten off.

Wind yarn around work approximately 0.5cm (¼in) from top to make a knot. Sew to shirt at neck edge. Catch down collar.

TROUSERS (make two pieces)

Using M and 1.25mm (#8) hook, make 16 ch, 1 dc in second ch from hook, 1 dc in each ch to end, 1 ch, turn (15 dc plus turning ch).

Work one row in dc.

Inc row 1 dc in first st (inc made), * 1 dc in next dc, 2 dc in next dc; rep from *, ending with 1 dc in turning ch, 1 ch, turn (23 dc plus turning ch).

Work 50 rows in dc, or until required length. Fasten off.

Measure against doll, mark crotch. Sew up the front, halfway up the back seam, and leg seams. Fit on doll, sew up rest of back seam. Run a length of thread through waist edge, pull up to fit.

NB Make the trousers slightly longer (approx 5–8 rows) if turn-ups are required.

JACKET

Using M and 1.25mm (#8) hook, make 22 ch, 1 dc in second ch from hook, 1 dc in each ch to end, 1 ch, turn (21 dc plus turning ch).

Work six rows in dc. Fasten off.

Work another piece to match but do not fasten off.

Next row Miss first st, dc to end, 1 dc in turning ch, work across the first piece in dc, 1 dc in turning ch, 1 ch, turn (43 dc plus turning ch).

Work 13 rows in dc.

Divide for armholes

Miss first st, 1 dc in next 10 dc, 1 ch, turn.

Work 10 rows in dc.

Next row Miss first st, 1 dc in next 7 dc, 1 ch, turn.

Work one row in dc. Fasten off.

Return to main piece, miss next 2 dc, rejoin yarn to the next dc with a sl st, 1 ch, 1 dc in next 17 dc, 1 ch, turn.

Work 12 rows in dc. Fasten off.

Return to main piece, miss next 2 dc, rejoin yarn to the next dc with a sl st, 1 ch, dc to end, 1 dc in turning ch, 1 ch, turn.

Work nine rows in dc.

Next row Miss first st, 1 dc in next 7 dc, 1 ch, turn. Work one row in dc. Fasten off. Sew up the shoulder seams.

Sleeves (make two)

Make 22 ch, 1 dc in second ch from hook, 1 dc in each ch to end, 1 ch, turn (21 dc plus turning ch).

Work 23 rows in dc or to length required. Fasten off.

Sew up sleeve seams, sew into armholes.

Collar

Work two rows in dc (approx. 20 sts) across both front and back neck edge. Fasten off.

Turn back the lapels on the fronts and catch down lightly. Sew on tiny buttons or beads to the front and on the sleeve cuffs. Fit on doll, add a stitch or two to keep jacket closed.

HAT

See Coat and Hat project (page 69).

PLUS-SIZE OUTFIT

Materials

One reel of DMC Broder Machine 30 in white for shirt

One-ply (approx 40 metres) for trousers

One-ply (approx 40 metres) for jumper

0.60, 1.25 and 1.50mm (US #14, #8 and #6) crochet hooks

Tiny beads or buttons for the shirt

SHIRT

Work back and fronts as one piece to the armhole. Using DMC Broder Machine 30 and 0.60mm (#14) hook, work 70 ch. 1 dc in second ch from hook, 1 dc in each ch, 1 ch, turn (69 dc plus turning ch).

Next row Miss first st, 1 dc in each dc, 1 dc in turning ch, 1 ch, turn.

Continue to work in rows of dc until work measures 2.5cm (1in).

Divide for armholes

First front

Miss first st, 1 dc in next 14 dc, 1 ch, turn.

Continue working rows of dc until work measures 4.5cm (1¾in), ending at the armhole edge.

Next row Miss first st, 1 dc in next 7 dc, 1 ch, turn.

Work four rows in dc. Fasten off.

Back

Return to main piece, miss the next 10 dc, rejoin thread to the next dc with a sl st, 1 ch, 1 dc in the next 19 dc, 1 ch, turn.

Continue working rows of dc until work measures same as first front. Fasten off.

Second front

Return to main piece, miss the next 10 dc, rejoin thread to the next dc with a sl st, 1 ch, dc to end, 1 dc in turning ch, 1 ch, turn (14 dc plus turning ch).

Continue working rows of dc until work measures 4.5cm (1¾in), working one row less than on first front, thereby ending at the armhole edge.

Next row Miss first st, 1 dc in next 7 dc, 1 ch, turn.

Work four rows in dc. Fasten off.

Sew up the shoulder seams.

Collar

With right side of work facing, rejoin thread to the fifth st at the neck edge on the right front with a sl st. 1 ch, work 32 dc across neck, ending with the last dc five sts in from the left front edge, 1 ch, turn.

Work one row in dc.

Inc row 1 dc in first st (inc made), 1 dc in each dc up to last dc, work 2 dc in this dc (inc made), 1 dc in turning ch, 1 ch, turn.

Work one row in dc.

Rep the last two rows three times (40 dc plus turning ch). Fasten off.

Sleeves (both alike)

With wrong side facing, rejoin thread at the centre underarm with a sl st, 1 ch, now work 50 dc around armhole edge, 1 ch, turn.

Next row Miss first st, dc to end, 1 dc in turning ch, 1 ch, turn.

Rep the last dc row three times.

Next row Miss first st, 1 dc in next st, dc 2 tog, dc to last 3 sts, dc 2 tog, 1 dc in last st, 1 dc in turning ch, 1 ch, turn.

Rep the last four rows until there are 42 dc plus turning ch.

Work three more rows in dc.

Next row Work the dec row once more.

Work one more row in dc.

Rep the last two rows until there are 30 dc plus turning ch.

Check measurement against doll and make any adjustments in length.

Next row Miss first st, 1 dc in next dc, dc 2 tog across row, ending with 1 dc in turning ch, 1 ch, turn (16 dc plus turning ch).

Work five rows in dc for the cuff. Fasten off.

Sew up half of the sleeve seam. Sew tiny beads or buttons to the shirt front and at the cuffs if required. Fit on doll, sew up the fronts, overlapping by approx five sts. Sew up the rest of the sleeve seam.

TROUSERS (Make two pieces)

Using one-ply yarn and 1.25mm (#8) hook, starting at the waist edge, work 25 ch. 1 dc in second ch from hook, 1 dc in each ch to end, 1 ch, turn (24 dc plus turning ch).

Work 18 rows in dc, working 4 ch at the end of the last row for the crotch, turn.

Next row 1 dc in second ch from hook, 1 dc in each ch, dc to end, 1 dc in turning ch, 4 ch, turn. Rep the last row once more, ending with 1 ch, turn.

Work 30 rows in dc, or to length required. Fasten off.

Measure approx. 2cm (¾in) from the side edge at the bottom of the leg. Thread a needle with yarn and work a row of chain stitches from bottom to top for a mock crease. Do the same on the other half of the leg.

JUMPER

Using one-ply yarn and 1.25mm (#8) hook, make 25 ch. 1 dc in second ch from hook, 1 dc in each ch to end, 1 ch, turn (24 dc plus turning ch).

Work three rows in dc, ending last row with 1 ch, turn.

Foundation row 2 tr in first st, * miss 2 dc, (1 dc, 2 tr) in next dc; rep from *, ending with miss 2 dc, 1 dc in turning ch, 1 ch, turn.

Pattern row 2 tr in first st, * miss 2 tr, (1 dc, 2 tr) in next dc; rep from *, ending with miss 2 tr, 1 dc in turning ch, 1 ch, turn.

Rep the pattern row for the length required.

Divide for neck

2 tr in first st, * miss 2 tr, (1 dc, 2 tr in next dc) twice, miss 2 tr, 1 dc in next dc, 1 ch, turn.

Cont working on these sts for 10 rows. Fasten off. Return to the main piece, miss the next (2 tr, 1 dc, 2 tr), rejoin yarn to the next dc with a sl st, 1 ch, 2 tr in same st, work in pattern to end.

Rep pattern row 11 times more, do not turn at end of last row.

Work 8 ch, (1 dc, 2 tr) in first st on the second side, work in pattern to end of row, 1 ch, turn.

Next row 2 tr in first st, (miss 2 tr, [1 dc, 2 tr] in next dc) three times, (miss 2 ch, [1 dc, 2 tr] in next ch) twice, miss 2 ch, (1 dc, 2 tr) in next dc, pattern to end, 1 ch, turn.

Work in pattern for length required.

Next row Miss first st, 1 dc in next and every st to end, 1 dc in turning ch, 1 ch, turn.

Work three more rows in dc. Fasten off.

Mark armholes, and sew up the side seams. Work a row of dc around armholes and neck.

HAT

See Coat and Hat project (page 69).

TIE

See Suit project (page 70).

DRESS SUIT

SHIRT

Make 25 ch, 1 dc in second ch from hook, 1 dc in each ch, 1 ch, turn.

Cont in dc until work measures approx. 4cm (1½in).

Divide for neck

Miss first st, 1 dc in next 7 dc, 1 ch, turn.

Work six rows in dc, working 9 ch at end of last row, turn.

** **Next row** Work 1 dc in second ch from hook, 1 dc in each ch, dc to end, 1 ch, turn.

Cont in dc until front measures same as back. Fasten off. **

Return to neck, miss the next 9 dc, rejoin thread to next dc with a sl st, 1 ch, dc to end, 1 ch, turn.

Work five rows in dc, working 9 ch at end of the last row, 1 ch, turn.

Rep from ** to **.

Collar

With right side facing, miss first 5 sts at neck edge on right front. Work 26 dc across neck, ending 5 sts from left front edge, 1 ch, turn.

Work one row in dc.

Work 10 rows in dc, working 1 dc in the first st on each row (inc made) (36 dc). Fasten off.

Sleeves (both alike)

With right side facing, starting 2.5cm (1in) from bottom edge, work 39 dc, ending 2.5cm (1in) from opposite bottom edge.

Work 14 rows in dc.

** **Dec row** Miss first st, dc 2 tog, work to the last 2 dc, dc 2 tog, 1 dc in turning ch, 1 ch, turn.

Work four more rows in dc. **

Rep from ** to ** until 31 sts remain. Cont in dc for length required.

Cuff

Miss first st, dc 2 tog across the row, 1 dc in

turning ch, 1 ch, turn.

Work five rows in dc. Fasten off.

Sew up side and half the sleeve seams, fit on doll, sew up the remaining sleeve seam. Sew on buttons or beads. Overlapping the first 5 sts, sew up the fronts.

Materials

One reel each of DMC Broder Machine 30 in two shades of grey for suit

Small amount in white for shirt

Small amount of contrast colour for waistcoat

Mini buttons for shirt, waistcoat and dress coat

Silk ribbon for top hat and corsage

Small piece of card to stiffen hat

0.60mm (US #14) crochet hook

TROUSERS (make two pieces)

Starting at the waist edge, make 26 ch, 1 dc in second ch from hook, 1 dc in each ch, 1 ch, turn. Work three rows in dc.

Next row Inc 8 sts evenly across row.

Cont in dc until work measures 4.5cm (1¾in) approx. Make 3 ch at end of the last row, turn.

Next row 1 dc in second ch from hook, 1 dc in next ch, dc to end, 3 ch, turn.

Rep the last row once more, ending with 1 ch, turn. Cont in dc for length required. Fasten off.

Sew up leg seams to the crotch, sew up front and half the back seam. Fit on doll, sew up rest of the back seam. Run two gathering threads at top and bottom of waist, pull up to fit.

NB I pressed creases in the trousers using a moderately hot iron before fitting on the doll.

WAISTCOAT (VEST)

Using contrast colour, make 54 ch, 1 dc in second ch from hook, 1 dc in each ch, 1 ch, turn. Work in dc for approx 2cm (¾in). Check measurement against the doll.

Next row Miss the first st, 1 dc in next 9 dc, 1 ch, turn.

Work three rows in dc.

* **Next row** Miss the first st, dc 2 tog, dc to end, 1 ch, turn.

Work three rows in dc.

Rep from * until the row 'miss first st, 1 dc in next 6 dc' has been worked. Work three rows in dc. Fasten off.

Return to armhole, miss the next 8 dc, rejoin thread to the next dc with a sl st, 1 ch, work in dc across the next 17 dc, 1 ch, turn.

Work 15 rows in dc. Fasten off.

Return to armhole, miss the next 8 dc, rejoin thread to the next dc with a sl st, 1 ch, dc to end, 1 ch, turn.

Work two rows in dc.

Next row Miss first st, dc 2 tog, dc to end, 1 ch, turn.

Work three rows in dc.

Cont as for the first front, ending with four rows

in dc. Fasten off.

Sew up shoulder seams, sew on mini buttons or beads. Fit on doll, overlap the fronts slightly, lightly tack the edges together.

CRAVAT

Make 10 ch, 1 dc in second ch from hook, 1 dc in each ch, 1 ch, turn.

Work 14 rows in dc.

Next row Miss first st, dc 2 tog, dc to end, 1 ch, turn.

Rep the last row seven times.

Work in dc on these two sts for approx 4.5cm (1¾in).

Next row 1 dc in first st, dc to end, 1 ch, turn (inc row).

Rep last row seven times.

Work 14 rows in dc. Fasten off.

Tie cravat around neck of doll, pushing bottom edges under waistcoat.

FROCK COAT

Right back

Make 11 ch, 1 dc in second ch from hook, 1 dc in each ch, 1 ch, turn (10 dc plus turning ch).

** **First inc row** 1 dc in first st (inc made), dc to end, 1 dc in turning ch, 1 ch, turn (11 dc).

Work one row in dc.

Second inc row 1 dc in first st (inc made), 1 dc in next 2 dc, 2 dc in next dc, dc to end, 1 dc in turning ch, 1 ch, turn (13 dc plus turning ch).

Work one row in dc.

Rep the last four rows seven times more, then the first inc row once more, break thread.

Left back

Work as for the right back, reversing shaping, i.e. work inc in the third last and last dc as appropriate, 1 dc in turning ch, 1 ch, turn. Do not break the thread on the final row, 1 ch, turn.

Work in dc across both left and right back, 1 ch, turn.

Inc row Miss first st, 2 dc in next dc (inc made), 1 dc in next 2 dc, 2 dc in next dc (inc made), dc to the last 4 dc, 2 dc in next dc (inc made), 1 dc in next 2 dc, 2 dc in next dc (inc made), 1 dc in turning ch, 1 ch, turn.

Work one row in dc.

Cont to work the first and second inc rows as before, inc sts. at both ends until there are 87 dc plus the turning ch, ending with the second inc row.

Work in dc until length required.

Divide for armholes

Right front

Miss first st, 1 dc in next 14 dc, 1 ch, turn.

Cont in dc until armhole measures approx 2cm (¾in), ending at armhole edge.

** **Next row** Miss first st, 1 dc in next 7 dc, 1 ch, turn.

Work five rows in dc. Fasten off. **

Back

Return to armhole edge, miss the next 14 dc, rejoin thread to the next dc with a sl st, 1 ch, 1 dc next 29 dc, 1 ch, turn.

Cont in dc until back measures same as front to shoulder. Fasten off.

Left front

Return to armhole edge, miss the next 14 dc, rejoin thread to the next dc with a sl st, 1 ch, dc to end, 1 dc in turning ch, 1 ch, turn.

Work in dc until left front measures same as right front to neck, ending at armhole edge.

Rep from ** to **.

Sew up shoulder seams.

Collar

Rejoin thread to fourth stitch at right front edge with a sl st, 1 ch, work 36 dc across neck edge, ending on fourth stitch from left edge.

Work nine rows in dc. Fasten off.

Turn over the front lapels and collar, catch down to hold.

Sleeves (both alike)

Rejoin thread at underarm with a sl st, 1 ch, work 46 dc around armhole edge, 1 ch, turn.

Work 10 rows in dc.

** **Dec row** Miss first st, dc 2 tog, dc to last 2 dc, dc 2 tog, 1 dc in turning ch, 1 ch, turn.

Work four rows in dc.

Rep from ** three times more, work the dec row once more.

Cont in dc for length required. Fasten off.

Sew up the sleeve seam, add buttons or beads and fit on doll. Make a corsage from a silk rose and greenery, glue to lapel.

TOP HAT

Crown

Make 4 ch, join into a ring with a sl st. 1 ch, work 9 dc into ring, sl st to join.

Next row 1 ch, 1 dc in each dc to end, sl st to join.

Rep last row once more.

Inc row 1 ch, 1 dc in same st, 2 dc in each dc to end, sl st to join.

Rep the dc row twice.

Rep the inc row once.

Cont in dc until hat is required height.

Brim

Rep the inc row once more.

Work in dc for five rows. Fasten off.

Stiffen hat with either spray starch or dilute PVA glue. Glue a length of ribbon around the base of the hat.

NB Make a former from polymer clay glued to a piece of wood, cover with foil, place the wet hat over this. Curve the brim, using pins for support until dry. Place a circle of card inside the hat for extra stiffening if needed.

5

PERSONAL ACCESSORIES

The designs in this chapter are primarily for the Victorian lady, although the beret and bag hail from more recent times. Lace collars have always been, and still are, a useful addition to a lady's wardrobe, ideal for dressing up a plain jumper. Fans were important accessories for the Victorian lady; I have included two different designs. The first is designed for a fan-shaped metal finding, the second for 1/12 scale fan sticks. Not as complicated to work as it looks, the last project in this chapter is a parasol, another vital accessory for a Victorian lady.

① ⑪ BERET AND SHOULDER BAG

One-ply yarn
(approx 30 metres)

1.25mm (US #8)
crochet hook

Button, bead or
jewellery finding for
bag

Small pompon for
beret

BERET ⑪

Make 30 ch.

First row 1 dc in second ch from hook, 1 dc in
each ch, 1 ch, turn (29 dc plus turning ch).
Work three rows in dc.

First inc row 1 dc in first st (inc made), 2 dc in
each dc to end, 1 ch, turn (59 dc plus turning ch).
Work two rows in dc.

Second inc row 1 dc in first st (inc made), * 2 dc
in next dc, 1 dc in next dc; rep from *, ending
with 2 dc in turning ch, 1 ch, turn (90 dc plus
turning ch).

Dec row Miss first st, * dc 2 tog, 1 dc in
rep from * to end, 1 ch, turn.

Rep the last dec row five times more.

Thread yarn through the rem 8 sts, pull
sew up seam. Make a tassel with seven pieces of
yarn and sew to top, or use a pompon.

SHOULDER BAG ①

Make 12 ch, work in dc for 5cm (2in). Fasten off.
Fold the bottom 2cm (¾in) and sew both side
seams. Sew on a mini button, jewellery finding or
bead for a fastening. Make a loop at the top and
fold over, slip loop over bead. Rejoin yarn to top
of one side seam with a sl st, work 30 ch, sl st to
top of second side seam. Fasten off.

LACE COLLAR 1

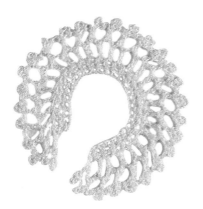

Make 28 ch, 1 dc in second ch from hook, 1 dc in each ch, 1 ch, turn (27 dc plus turning ch).
Work one row in dc, 6 ch, turn.
Next row Miss first st, 1 tr in next dc, * 3 ch, 1 tr in next dc; rep from *, ending with 3 ch, 1 tr in turning ch, 6 ch, turn.

Edging

1 dc into third ch from hook, * 2 ch, 1 tr in next 3 ch space, 4 ch, 1 dc into the top of the tr just worked; rep from *, ending with 2 ch, 1 tr into the third of the 6 turning ch, 4 ch, sl st in top of tr. Fasten off.

Materials

Small amount of DMC Broder Machine 30

0.60mm (US #14) crochet hook

LACE COLLAR 2

Make 25 ch, 1 dc in second ch from hook, 1 dc in each ch, 3 ch, turn (24 dc plus turning ch).
Next row Miss first st, 1 dc in next dc, * 2 ch, 1 dc in next dc; rep from *, ending with 2 ch, 1 dc in turning ch, 3 ch, turn.
Next row 1 dc in first 2 ch space, * 2 ch, 1 dc in next 2 ch space; rep from * to end, 3 ch, turn.

Edging

4 tr in 2 ch space, * 1 dc in next 2 ch space, 5 tr in next 2 ch space; rep from *, ending with 1 dc in 2 ch space, 4 tr in last ch space, 1 tr in first ch of previous row. Fasten off.

Materials

Small amount of DMC Broder Machine 30

0.60mm (US #14) crochet hook

FAN 1

Materials

Small amount of DMC
Broder Machine 30

0.60mm (US #14)
crochet hook

White PVA glue

7.5cm (3in) of 2mm
silk ribbon

Small gold-coloured
metal fan (see List of
Suppliers, page 114)

Make 28 ch.

Foundation row 2 tr in third ch from hook, miss 4 ch, * 5 tr in next ch (shell made), miss 4 ch; rep from *, ending with 3 tr in last ch, 3 ch, turn.

First pattern row 2 tr in first st, * 5 tr in centre of next 5 tr shell (shell made); rep from *, ending with 3 tr in turning ch, 3 ch, turn.

Second pattern row 3 tr in first st, * 6 tr in centre of next 5 tr shell (shell made); rep from *, ending with 4 tr in turning ch. Fasten off.

Gather the ch edge slightly to fit metal fan, glue to the fan with white PVA glue. Fold the ribbon in half, pull through hole in fan and knot to secure.

FAN 2

Centre pattern Make 6 ch, (2 tr, 3 ch, 2 tr) into the sixth ch from hook, 5 ch, turn.
Pattern row (2 tr, 3 ch, 2 tr) in the 3 ch space, 5 ch, turn.
Rep the pattern row 12 times more, omitting the last 5 ch. Do not turn, do not break thread.

Heading
Work 7 dc in the first 5 ch loop, cont to work 7 dc in each 5 ch loop across the row, ending with 3 dc in the last loop. Fasten off.
Top edge, row 1 rejoin thread to the first 5 ch loop on the second side, 6 ch, (1 tr, 2 ch) 3 times in this 5 ch loop, 1 tr in the same loop, * 3 ch, (1 tr, 2 ch) 4 times in the next 5 ch loop, 1 tr in the same loop; rep from *, ending with 4 ch, turn.

Row 2 1 tr in the first ch space, (1 ch, 2 tr in the next ch space) 3 times, * miss the next 3 ch space, 2 tr in the next 2 ch space, (1 ch, 2 tr in the next ch space) 3 times; rep from * to end. Fasten off. Glue the crochet to the fan sticks. Make a tiny tassel and attach to the bottom of the fan stick using a very fine needle.

Materials

Small amount of DMC Broder Machine 30

0.60mm (US #14) crochet hook

White PVA glue

Fan sticks (see List of Suppliers, page 114)

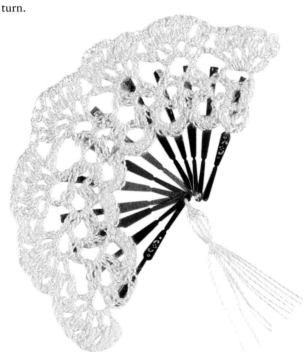

PARASOL

One reel of DMC Broder Machine 30

0.60mm (US #14) crochet hook

Cocktail stick and glass bead for handle

Silk ribbon

Large bar filigree (six)

Small bead, jewellery finding, or egg-decorating finding (see List of Suppliers, page 114)

Make 6 ch, join into a ring with a sl st. 3 ch, work 11 tr into ring, sl st to top of 3 ch to join.
First row 3 ch, 5 tr into same st, miss next tr, * 6 tr into next tr, miss next tr; rep from * all round, sl st to top of 3 ch to join (6 shells made).
Second row * 6 tr in centre of shell, 1 dc in space between shells; rep from *, ending last rep with a sl st to join to first dc.
Third row 8 ch, 1 dc into same st, * 6 tr into next 6 tr shell (shell made), 1 dc into next dc, 8 ch, 1 dc into same st; rep from *, ending with 6 tr into 6 tr shell (shell made), sl st into base of first 8 ch loop.
Fourth row sl st to centre of 8 ch loop, 8 ch, 1 dc

into same loop, * 6 ch, 1 dc into centre of 6 tr shell, 6 ch, 1 dc into 8 ch loop, 8 ch, 1 dc into same loop; rep from *, ending last rep with a sl st into base of first 8 ch loop.
NB it is helpful to place a coloured marker at beginning of last row.
Fifth row sl st to centre of 8 ch loop, 8 ch, 1 dc in same loop, * (6 ch, 1 dc into centre of next 6 ch space) twice, 6 ch, 1 dc into centre of 8 ch loop, 8 ch, 1 dc into same loop; rep from *, ending with a sl st into base of first 8 ch loop.
Sixth row sl st to centre of 8 ch loop, 8 ch, 1 dc in same loop, * (6 ch, 1 dc into centre of next 6 ch space) three times, 6 ch, 1 dc into centre of

8 ch loop, 8 ch, 1 dc into same loop; rep from *, ending with a sl st into base of first 8 ch loop.

Seventh row sl st to centre of 8 ch loop, 8 ch, 1 dc in same loop, * (6 ch, 1 dc into centre of next 6 ch space) four times, 6 ch, 1 dc into centre of 8 ch loop, 8 ch, 1 dc into same loop; rep from *, ending with a sl st into base of first 8 ch loop.

Eighth row sl st to centre of 8 ch loop, 8 ch, 1 dc into same loop, * (6 ch, 1 dc in next 6 ch space) twice, 6 tr in next 6 ch space, 1 dc in next 6 ch space, 6 ch, 1 dc in next 6 ch space, 6 ch, 1 dc in next 8 ch loop, 8 ch, 1 dc in same loop; rep from *, ending last rep with a sl st into base of first 8 ch loop.

Ninth row sl st to centre of 8 ch loop, 8 ch, 1 dc into same loop, * (6 ch, 1 dc into next 6 ch space) twice, 6 ch, 1 dc into centre of 6 tr, (6 ch, 1 dc in next 6 ch space) twice, 6 ch, 1 dc in 8 ch loop, 8 ch, 1 dc in same loop; rep from *, ending last rep with a sl st into base of first 8 ch loop.

Tenth row sl st to centre of 8 ch loop, 8 ch, 1 dc into same loop, * 6 ch, 1 dc in next 6 ch space, 6 tr in next 6 ch space, 1 dc in next 6 ch space, 8 ch, 1 dc in next 6 ch space, 6 tr in next 6 ch space, 1 dc in next 6 ch space, 6 ch, 1 dc in 8 ch

loop, 8 ch, 1 dc in same loop; rep from *, ending last rep with a sl st into base of first 8 ch loop.

Eleventh row sl st to centre of 8 ch loop, 8 ch, 1 dc into same loop, * 6 ch, 1 dc in next 6 ch space, 6 ch, 1 dc in centre of 6 tr, 6 ch, 1 dc in next 8 ch space, 6 ch, 1 dc in centre of 6 tr, 6 ch, 1 dc in next 6 ch space, 6 ch, 1 dc in next 8 ch loop; rep from *, ending with a sl st into base of first 8 ch loop.

Twelfth row * (8 ch, 1 dc into 8 ch loop) 4 times, (6 ch, 1 dc in next 6 ch space) 6 times, 6 ch, 1 dc in next 8 ch loop; rep from *, ending with a sl st into base of the first 8 ch loop. Fasten off. Sew in ends.

Making up the parasol

Lightly cover the cocktail stick with white PVA glue, twist the silk ribbon around the stick to cover, ending approx 1.25cm (½in) from the top. Glue the glass bead to the opposite end of the cocktail stick. Glue the long bar filigrees to the uncovered part of the cocktail stick, spreading them out evenly. When dry, glue crochet to the filigree bars. Finish top of parasol with the small bead or finding.

6

HOUSEHOLD ITEMS

Until the advent of electric blankets, the only way to warm a bed was with either a warming pan or a pottery hot-water bottle, which pre-dated the rubberized type. Treat your hot-water bottle to a stylish cover; like the tea cosy and shopping bag, it is very quick and easy to make. Every home needs cushions; I have designed a pair of very simple ones in one-ply yarn, as well as the more challenging pair in cotton.

In Victorian times when Macassar hair oil was popular, chairs and sofas had covers (antimacassars) placed on the backs to prevent the oil from ruining the chair fabric. Some of these antimacassars were highly decorated with embroidery. I have created a set in crochet that would look very stylish in any setting, but especially so in a Victorian drawing room.

Crochet bedspreads have always been popular. The one included here would look lovely in any setting, from Victorian times through to the present day. Place mats make a table setting look extra special; you could add an extra glass mat to make a chervil set for my lady's dressing table. Every bedside cabinet should have a glass jug, and every jug should have a beaded cover to keep away flies and other insects.

Dolls' houses need curtains. I have designed a pair of curtains suitable for most rooms in the house, and a café-style curtain. The latter can be lengthened to cover the entire window. The final design in this chapter is for a round tablecloth; I consider this to be the most challenging project in the book.

① TEA COSY

Make two pieces

Make 18 ch.

Foundation row 2 dc in fourth ch from hook, * miss 1 ch, 2 dc in next ch; rep from *, ending with 2 ch, turn.

Pattern row 2 dc in second st, * miss 1 st, 2 dc in next st; rep from *, ending with 2 ch, turn.

Rep last row 11 times more, or to length required.

Dec row Work 2 dc tog across row.

Rep last row once more. Fasten off.

Sew up the side seams, leaving gaps for handle and spout. Run a gathering thread through the top edge, pull up to fit. Glue a small pompon to the top.

① HOT-WATER BOTTLE COVER

Make two pieces

Make 13 ch.

Foundation row Work 3 dc in third ch from hook, * miss 2 ch, work 3 dc in next ch; rep from *, ending with 1 dc in last ch, 1 ch, turn.

Pattern row Work 3 dc in second dc of each 3 dc group, ending with 1 dc in turning ch, 1 ch, turn.

Rep the pattern row 12 times, or to length required. Fasten off.

Sew up the side and bottom seams, slip the hot-water bottle inside and run a gathering thread around neck of bottle, pull up to fit, tie ends into a bow.

SHOPPING BAG

Materials

Small amount of one-ply yarn

1.00mm (US #10) crochet hook

Work the back and front as one piece.

Make 17 ch, 1 dc in second ch from hook, 1 dc in each ch, 3 ch, turn.

First pattern row Miss first st, 1 tr in next dc, * 1 ch, miss 1 dc, 1 tr in next 2 dc; rep from *, ending with 1 tr in turning ch, 1 ch, turn.

Second pattern row Miss first st, 1 dc in each dc and 1 ch space, ending with 1 dc in turning ch, 3 ch, turn.

Rep the last two rows until work measures 7.5 cm (3in), or length required. Fasten off.

Sew up the side seams.

Handle

Rejoin yarn with a sl st to top of bag approx 1cm (⅜in) from the side, work 20 ch, sl st to join 1cm (⅜in) from opposite side.

Work a second handle to match.

AFGHAN

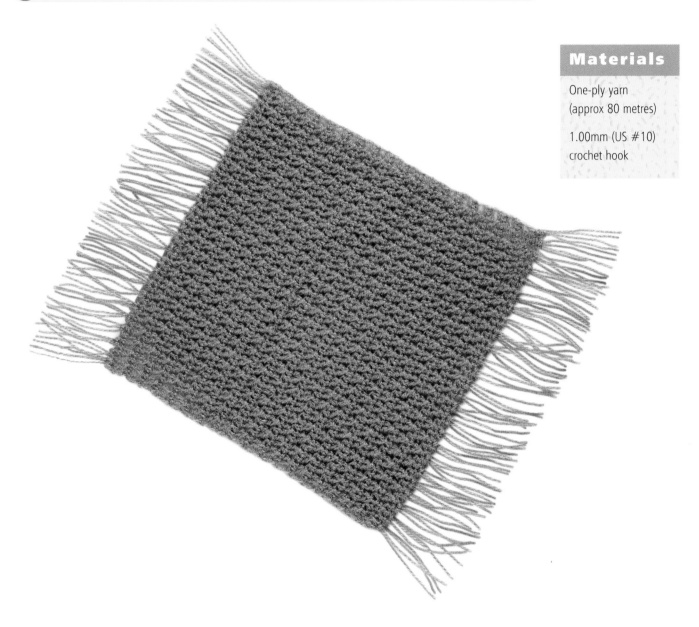

Materials

One-ply yarn
(approx 80 metres)

1.00mm (US #10)
crochet hook

Make 50 ch.

Foundation row 1 dc in second ch from hook,
1 dc in each ch, 3 ch, turn.

First pattern row Miss first st, * miss next dc,
1 tr in next dc, 1 tr in missed dc; rep from *,
ending with 1 tr in turning ch, 1 ch, turn.

Second pattern row Miss first st, 1 dc in each tr,
ending with 1 dc in turning ch, 3 ch, turn.

Rep the two pattern rows for length required.
Fasten off.

Fringe

Cut yarn into 6cm (2¼in) lengths. Working across
ch row and last dc row, knot two lengths of yarn
together for the fringe.

Four Cushions

 ## SQUARE CUSHION 1

Materials

Small amount of one-ply yarn

1.00mm (US #10) crochet hook

Polyester stuffing

Make 16 ch.

Foundation row 1 tr into fifth ch from hook, 1 tr in previous (fourth) ch, * miss next ch, 1 tr in next ch, 1 tr in missed ch; rep from * to end, 3 ch, turn.

Pattern row Miss first 2 sts, 1 tr in next st, 1 tr in previous st, * miss next st, 1 tr in next st, 1 tr in missed st; rep from * to end, 3 ch, turn.

Rep the pattern row until work measures 5cm (2in). Fasten off.

Fold in half and sew up two of the seams. Stuff lightly before sewing the third seam.

① ROUND CUSHION

Materials

Small amount of one-ply yarn in two colours, A and B

1.00mm (US #10) crochet hook

Polyester stuffing

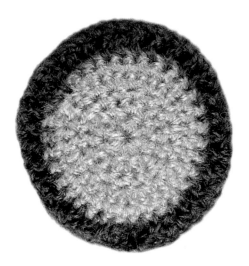

Make two pieces

Using A, make 4 ch, sl st to join into a ring.

Next row 1 ch, work 7 dc into the ring, sl st to join.

Next row 1 ch, 1 dc in same st, 2 dc in each dc to end, sl st to join.

Next row 1 ch, 1 dc in each dc, sl st to join.

Rep the last two rows once more, break A.

Next row Join in B with a sl st, work 3 ch, * 1 tr into next dc, 1 ch; rep from * to end, sl st to join. Fasten off.

With wrong sides together, join both pieces tog with a row of dc, stuff lightly when three quarters of the row has been worked, dc to end. Fasten off.

SQUARE CUSHION 2

Using A, make 23 ch.

Foundation row 1 dc in second ch from hook, * 3 ch, 1 tr in same ch as dc, miss 2 ch, 1 dc in next ch; rep from * to end, turn, cut thread.

First pattern row Using B, 3 ch, 1 tr into first st, 1 dc into next 3 ch space, * 3 ch, 1 tr into same 3 ch space, 1 dc into next 3 ch space; rep from *, ending with 2 ch, 1 tr in first dc of previous row, miss turning ch, turn, cut thread.

Second pattern row Using C, 1 ch, 1 dc into first st, 3 ch, 1 tr into next 2 ch space, * (1 dc, 3 ch, 1 tr) in next 3 ch space; rep from *, ending with 1 dc into top of turning ch, turn, cut thread.

Cont in this manner, changing colours on every row until row 23 has been worked, or for length required. Fasten off.

Sew up two of the three seams, stuff lightly, sew up the remaining seam.

Materials

A small amount of Gütermann silk thread in three colours, A, B and C

0.60mm (US #14) crochet hook

Polyester stuffing

SQUARE CUSHION 3

Do not cut the thread after each colour change. Using A, make 22 ch.

Foundation row Work 3 dc into third ch from hook, * miss 2 ch, 3 dc in next ch; rep from * to end, working one dc in last ch, change to B, 1 ch, turn.

Pattern row 3 dc in second dc of each 3 dc group, ending with 1 dc in last st (turning ch on subsequent rows).

Rep last row once more, changing to colour A before the final turning ch.

Work two rows in A, changing colour back to B before the final turning ch on the second row. Cont changing colour after every two pattern rows until 36 rows have been worked (18 colour changes), or to length required. Fasten off, finish as Square Cushion 2.

Materials

Small amount of Madeira Tanne Cotona 30 in two colours, A and B

0.60mm (US #14) crochet hook

Polyester stuffing

BEDSPREAD

Materials

One ball of Southern Comfort (sufficient for two)

1.75mm (US #4) crochet hook

Make 50 ch.

Foundation row 1 dc in second ch from hook, * miss 2 ch, (1 tr [1 ch 1 tr] 4 times) in next ch, miss 2 ch, 1 dc in next ch; rep from * to end of row, 5 ch, turn.

First pattern row * 1 dc in second 1 ch space, 1 ch 1 dc in third 1 ch space, 2 ch 1 tr in dc, 2 ch; rep from *, ending with 1 tr, 1 ch, turn.

Second pattern row 1 dc in first st, * (1 tr [1 ch 1 tr] 4 times) in

1 ch space, 1 dc in tr; rep from *, ending with 1 dc in turning ch, 5 ch, turn.

Rep the two pattern rows 17 times more, or for length required.

Edging

Work the second pattern row at side edge, a row of dc at top edge and the second pattern row on the second side edge. Fasten off.

PLACE MATS

Materials

Small amount of DMC
Broder Machine 30

0.60mm (US #14)
crochet hook

To make a cluster

Half-work the next 3 tr by leaving the last loop
from each tr on hook, thread over hook, pull
through all the sts to create one st; this makes a
3 tr cluster.

GLASS MAT

Make 6 ch, join into a ring with a sl st. 3 ch,
11 tr into ring, sl st to top of 3 ch to join.

First row 3 ch, half-work the next two tr, thread
over hook and pull through all loops (counts as
first cluster), * 2 ch, make a cluster in next loop;
rep from * all round, 2 ch, sl st to top of first
cluster made.

Second row 3 ch, 4 tr in same st, * 3 ch, 1 dc in
next cluster, 3 ch, 5 tr in next cluster; rep from *,
ending with 3 ch, sl st to the top of the first 3 ch.
Fasten off.

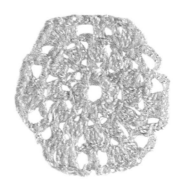

TABLE MAT

Work as for the glass mat to end of second row.

Third row sl st to centre of the 5 tr group, 3 ch,
4 tr in the same st, * 3 ch, 1 dc in last tr of group,
3 ch, 1 dc in next dc, 3 ch, 1 dc in first tr of next
5 tr group, 3 ch, 5 tr in centre tr of same group;
rep from *, ending the last rep by omitting the
last 5 tr, sl st to top of first 3 ch.

Fourth row sl st to centre of 5 tr group, 3 ch,
(2 tr, 2 ch, 3 tr) in same st, * (3 ch, 1 dc in next
ch space) 4 times, 3 ch, (3 tr, 2 ch, 3 tr) in centre
tr of 5 tr group; rep from *, ending the last rep by
omitting the (3 tr, 2 ch, 3 tr) in centre of 5 tr
group, sl st to top of first 3 ch.

Fifth row sl st to 2 ch space, * 4 ch, 1 dc in next
3 ch space, (3 ch, 1 dc in next 3 ch space) 4 times,
4 ch, 1 dc in next 2 ch space; rep from *, ending
the last rep with 4 ch, sl st to first of 4 ch.
Fasten off.

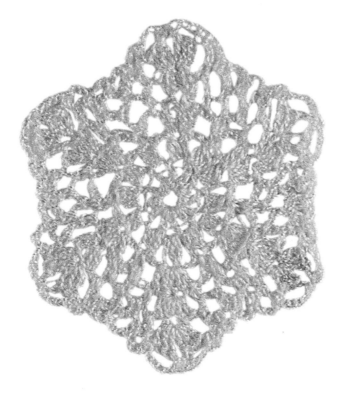

BEADED JUG COVER

Materials

Small amount of DMC Broder Machine 30

0.60mm (US #14) crochet hook

18 seed beads

To make a cluster

Half-work the next 3 (4) tr by leaving the last loop from each tr on hook, thread over hook, pull through all the sts to create one st; this makes a 3 (4) tr cluster

NB Thread beads onto the thread before commencing the crochet. Alternatively, the beads can be sewn on after the crochet has been completed.

Make 6 ch, join into a ring with a sl st.

First row 6 ch, * (1 tr, 2 ch) into ring; rep from * 6 times more, sl st to the fourth ch to join.

Second row sl st to centre of first 2 ch space, 3 ch, work a 3 tr cluster, * 5 ch, work a 4 tr cluster in the next ch space; rep from *, ending with 5 ch, sl st to top of first cluster made.

Third row * 5 ch, 1 dc in next 5 ch loop, 5 ch, 1 dc in top of next cluster; rep from *, ending with a sl st in first ch worked.

Fourth row sl st to centre of first 5 ch space, 3 ch, work a 3 tr cluster, * 6 ch, work a 4 tr cluster in next ch space; rep from *, ending with 6 ch, sl st into top of first cluster made.

Fifth row sl st to centre of first 6 ch space, 1 dc, * 3 ch, slip a seed bead up to the hook, 1 ch to enclose bead, 2 ch, 1 dc in the next 6 ch space; rep from *, ending with a sl st into the first dc. Fasten off.

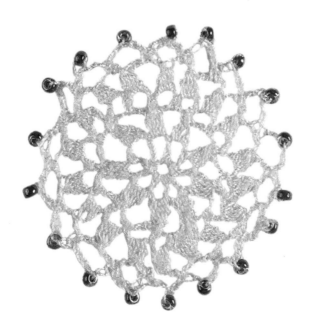

ANTIMACASSARS

Materials

One reel of DMC
Broder Machine 50

0.60mm (US #14)
crochet hook

CHAIR (make two)

Make 33 ch.

Foundation row Work 1 tr in third ch from
hook, * miss 2 ch, 1 tr in next ch, miss 2 ch, 5 tr
in next ch; rep from *, ending with 3 tr in last ch,
3 ch, turn.

First pattern row 2 tr in first st, * 1 tr in single tr,
5 tr in centre of shell; rep from *, ending with 3 tr
in turning ch, 3 ch, turn.

Second pattern row 1 tr in first st, miss next
2 sts, * 1 tr in next tr, 5 tr in centre shell; rep
from *, ending with 3 tr in turning ch, 3 ch, turn.
Rep the two pattern rows 10 times, or for length
required. Fasten off.

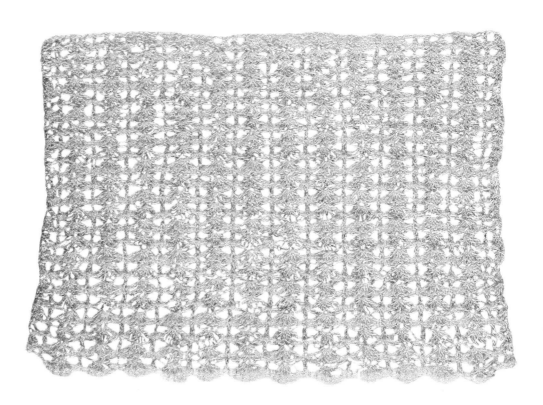

SETTEE/SOFA

Make 75 ch.

Follow pattern as for chair.

NB Use DMC Broder Machine 30 if preferred;
this will give a slightly larger piece.

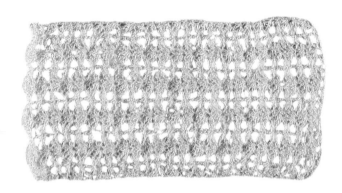

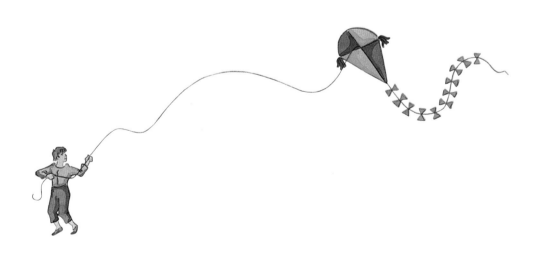

⑪ CURTAINS AND TIES

Materials

One-ply yarn
(approx 200 metres)

1.50mm (US #6)
crochet hook

Curtain pole

CURTAINS (make two)

Make 52 ch. (The pattern is worked in multiples of 2 ch. Thus, if you require a wider curtain, add another 2 ch for each complete pattern required. Instructions are for a window about 4½–5in (11–12.5cm) wide, 5–6in (12.5–15cm) deep.)

Foundation row 1 dc into fourth ch from hook, 1 tr in next ch, * 1 dc in next ch, 1 tr in next ch; rep from *, ending with 1 dc in last ch, 3 ch, turn.

Pattern row Miss first st, * 1 dc into next tr, 1 tr into next dc; rep from *, ending with 1 dc in top of turning ch, 3 ch, turn.

Rep the pattern row 74 times more, or until the length required. Fasten off.

Run a gathering thread approximately one third of the way from bottom edge of curtain, pull up into gathers, fasten off securely. (If you require your curtain to close, omit the gathering thread.)

Fold over the top of the curtain and catch down, enclosing the curtain pole.

TIES (make two)

Work 40 ch, 1 dc in second ch from hook, 1 dc in each ch to end, 1 ch, turn.

Work one row in dc, ending with 5 ch, turn.

Miss first st, 1 dc in next st, * 5 ch, miss next st, 1 dc in next st; rep from *, ending with the last dc in the turning ch, 6 ch.

Work back along the initial ch edge as follows: 1 dc in the first ch, * 5 ch, miss the next ch, 1 dc in the next ch; rep from *, ending with the last dc in the final ch, 6 ch, sl st to the base of the first 5 ch space. Fasten off.

Fold the tie in half over the gathered part of the curtain, and work a few sts to hold it securely in place.

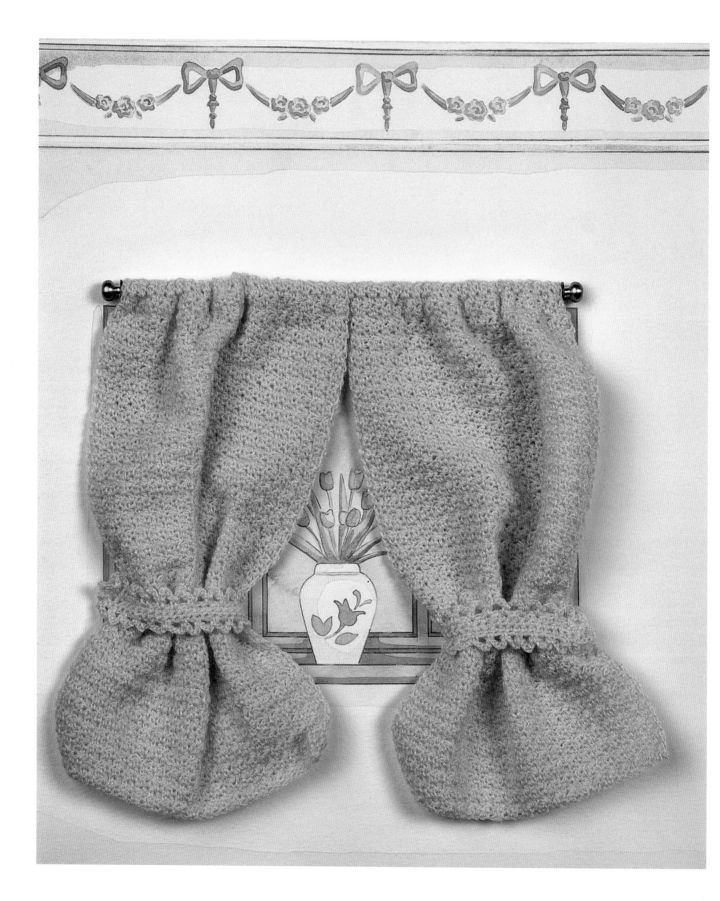

CAFÉ-STYLE CURTAIN

Starting at the top of curtain with the casing, make 150 ch. (The pattern is worked in multiples of 12 ch, plus 3, plus 3 turning ch. Thus, if you require a wider curtain, add another 12 ch to the above for each complete pattern required. The instructions suit a window about 4½–5in (11–12.5cm) wide.)

First row 1 tr in third ch from hook, 1 tr in each ch to end, 3 ch, turn.

Work 6 rows in tr, ending last row with 3 ch, turn.

Foundation row Miss first st, 1 tr in next 2 tr, * 2 ch, miss next 2 tr, 1 tr in next tr, 2 ch, miss next 2 tr, 1 tr in next tr, 3 ch, miss next 2 tr, 1 dc in next tr, 3 ch, miss next 2 tr, 1 tr in next tr; rep from *, working 3 tr in last 2 tr, 1 tr in turning ch, 3 ch, turn.

First pattern row Miss first st, 1 tr in next 2 tr, * 5 ch, 1 tr in next tr, 3 ch, 1 dc in next tr, 3 ch, 1 tr in next tr; rep from *, ending with 1 tr in last tr, 1 tr in turning ch, 3 ch, turn.

Second pattern row Miss first st, 1 tr in next 2 tr, * 5 ch, 1 tr in next tr, 2 ch, 1 tr in centre ch of 5 ch space, 2 ch, 1 tr in next tr; rep from *, ending with 1 tr in last tr, 1 tr in turning ch, 3 ch, turn.

Third pattern row Miss first st, 1 tr in next 2 tr, * 3 ch, 1 dc in next tr, 3 ch, 1 tr in next tr, 2 ch, 1 tr in centre ch of 5 ch space, 2 ch, 1 tr in next tr; rep from *, ending with 1 tr in last tr, 1 tr in turning ch, 3 ch, turn.

Fourth pattern row Miss first st, 1 tr in next 2 tr, * 3 ch, 1 dc in next tr, 3 ch, 1 tr in next tr, 5 ch, 1 tr in next tr; rep from *, ending with 1 tr in last tr, 1 tr in turning ch, 3 ch, turn.

Materials

One reel of DMC Broder Machine 30

0.60mm (US #14) crochet hook

Curtain pole

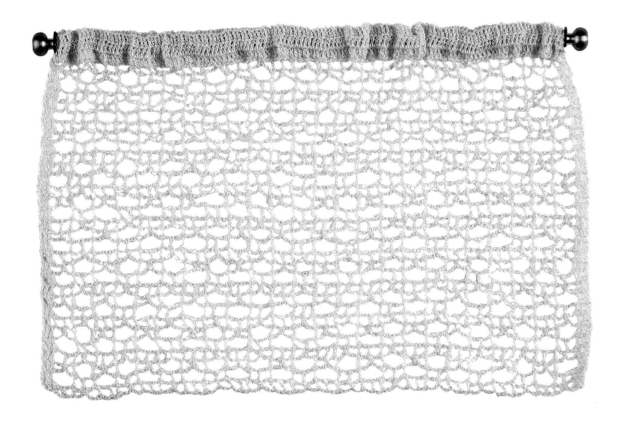

Fifth pattern row Miss first st, 1 tr in next 2 tr, * 2 ch, 1 tr in centre ch of 5 ch space, 2 ch, 1 tr in next tr, 5 ch, 1 tr in next tr; rep from *, ending with 1 tr in last tr, 1 tr in turning ch, 3 ch, turn.

Sixth pattern row Miss first st, 1 tr in next 2 tr, * 2 ch, 1 tr in centre ch of 5 ch space, 2 ch, 1 tr in next tr, 3 ch, 1 dc in next tr, 3 ch, 1 tr in next tr; rep from *, ending with 1 tr in last tr, 1 tr in turning ch, 3 ch, turn.

These six rows form the pattern; rep for the length required. I worked five pattern repeats to measure half the depth of the window.

Fasten off.

Fold over the top of the curtain and catch it down, enclosing the curtain pole. Arrange the gathers evenly.

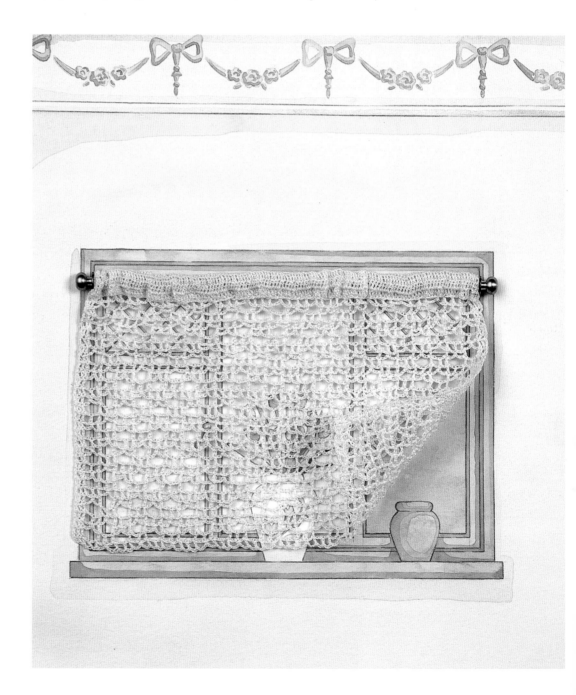

TABLECLOTH

Materials

DMC Broder Machine 30, 300m reel

0.60mm (US #14) crochet hook

Make 8 ch, join into a ring with a sl st. 1 ch, 11 dc into ring, sl st to join.

Row 1 3 ch, 1 tr into same st, * 2 tr into next st; rep from *, sl st to join (23 tr plus turning ch).

Row 2 4 ch, * 1 dc in each of next 4 sts, 4 ch; rep from *, ending with 1 dc in last 3 sts, sl st to base of 4 ch to join.

Row 3 sl st to centre of the first 4 ch, 3 ch, 4 tr in same 4 ch space, 3 ch, * 5 tr in next 4 ch space, 3 ch; rep from *, sl st into top of first 3 ch to join.

Row 4 3 ch, 1 tr in same st, 1 tr in next tr, 2 tr in next tr, 1 tr in next tr, 2 tr in last tr of group, 4 ch, * 2 tr in first tr of next 5 tr group, 1 tr in next tr, 2 tr in next tr, 1 tr in next tr, 2 tr in last tr of group, 4 ch; rep from *, sl st to top of first 3 ch to join.

Row 5 3 ch, (1 tr, 3 ch, 2 tr) in same st, (2 tr, 3 ch, 2 tr) in centre tr of same group, (2 tr, 3 ch, 2 tr) in last tr of same group, * (2 tr, 3 ch, 2 tr) in first tr of next group, (2 tr, 3 ch, 2 tr) in centre tr

of same group, (2 tr, 3 ch, 2 tr) in last tr of same group; rep from *, sl st to top of 3 ch to join.

Row 6 sl st to centre of first 3 ch space, 3 ch, (1 tr, 3 ch, 2 tr) in same space, 2 ch, * (2 tr, 3 ch, 2 tr) in next 3 ch space, 2 ch; rep from *, ending with a sl st into top of first 3 ch to join.

Row 7 sl st to centre of first 3 ch space, 3 ch, (1 tr, 3 ch, 2 tr) in same 3 ch space, 4 ch, * miss next 2 ch space, (2 tr, 3 ch, 2 tr) in next 3 ch space, 4 ch; rep from *, sl st to top of first 3 ch to join.

Row 8 sl st to centre of first 3 ch space, 3 ch, (1 tr, 3 ch, 2 tr) in same 3 ch space, 6 ch, * miss next 4 ch space, (2 tr, 3 ch, 2 tr) in next 3 ch space, 6 ch; rep from *, sl st to top of first 3 ch to join.

Row 9 sl st to centre of first 3 ch space, 3 ch, (1 tr, 3 ch, 2 tr) in same space, 3 ch, 1 dc in next 6 ch space, 3 ch, * (2 tr, 3 ch, 2 tr) in next 3 ch space, 3 ch, 1 dc in next 6 ch space, 3 ch; rep from *, ending with a sl st in top of first 3 ch.

Row 10 sl st to centre of first 3 ch space, 3 ch, (1 tr, 3 ch, 2 tr) in same space, 4 ch, 1 dc in next dc, 4 ch, * (2 tr, 3 ch, 2 tr) in 3 ch space between trebles, 4 ch, 1 dc in next dc, 4 ch; rep from *, ending with a sl st in top of first 3 ch.

Row 11 sl st to centre of first 3 ch space, 3 ch, (1 tr, 3 ch, 2 tr) in same space, (4 ch, 1 dc in next 4 ch space) twice, 4 ch, * (2 tr, 3 ch, 2 tr) in next 3 ch space, (4 ch, 1 dc, in next 4 ch space) twice; rep from *, ending with a sl st in top of first 3 ch.

Row 12 sl st to centre of first 3 ch space, 3 ch, (1 tr, 3 ch, 2 tr) in same space, 6 ch, miss next 4 ch space, 1 dc in next 4 ch space, 6 ch, miss next 4 ch space, * (2 tr, 3 ch, 2 tr) in next 3 ch space, 6 ch, miss next 4 ch space, 1 dc in next 4 ch space, 6 ch, miss next 4 ch space; rep from *, ending with a sl st in top of first 3 ch.

Row 13 sl st to centre of first 3 ch space, 3 ch, (1 tr, 3 ch, 2 tr) in same space, 6 ch, 1 dc in next dc, 6 ch, * (2 tr, 3 ch, 2 tr) in next 3 ch space, 6 ch, 1 dc in next dc, 6 dc; rep from *, ending with a sl st in top of first 3 ch.

Row 14 sl st to centre of first 3 ch space, 3 ch, (1 tr, 3 ch, 2 tr) in same space, (6 ch, 1 dc in next 6 ch space) twice, 6 ch, * (2 tr, 3 ch, 2 tr) in next 3 ch space, (6 ch, 1 dc in next 6 ch space) twice, 6 ch; rep from *, ending with a sl st in top of first 3 ch.

Row 15 sl st to centre of first 3 ch space, 3 ch, (1 tr, 3 ch, 2 tr) in same space, 7 ch, miss next 6 ch space, 1 dc in next 6 ch space, 7 ch, miss next 6 ch space, * (2 tr, 3 ch, 2 tr) in next 3 ch space, 7 ch, miss next 6 ch space, 1 dc in next 6 ch space, 7 ch; rep from *, ending with a sl st in top of first 3 ch.

Row 16 sl st to centre of the first 3 ch space, 3 ch, (1 tr, 3 ch, 2 tr) in the same space, 7 ch, 1 dc in the next dc, 7 ch, * (2 tr, 3 ch, 2 tr) in the next 3 ch space, 7 ch, 1 dc in the next dc, 7 ch; rep from *, ending with a sl st in the top of the first 3 ch.

Row 17 sl st to the centre of the first 3 ch space, 3 ch, (1 tr, 3 ch, 2 tr) in the same space, (8 ch, 1 dc in the next 7 ch space) twice, 8 ch, * (2 tr, 3 ch, 2 tr) in the next 3 ch space, (8 ch, 1 dc in the next 7 ch) twice, 8 ch; rep from *, ending with a sl st in the top of the first 3 ch.

Row 18 sl st to the centre of the first 3 ch space, 3 ch, (1 tr, 3 ch, 2 tr) in the same space, 8 ch, miss the next 8 ch space, 1 dc in the next 8 ch space, 8 ch, miss the next 8 ch space, * (2 tr, 3 ch, 2 tr) in the next 3 ch space, 8 ch, miss the next 8 ch space, 1 dc in the next 8 ch space, 8 ch; rep from *, ending with a sl st in the top of the first 3 ch.

Row 19 sl st to the centre of the first 3 ch space, 3 ch, (1 tr, 3 ch, 2 tr) in the same space, 8 ch, 1 dc in the next dc, 8 ch, * (2 tr, 3 ch, 2 tr) in the next 3 ch space, 8 ch, 1 dc in the next dc, 8 ch; rep from *, ending with a sl st in the top of the first 3 ch.

Row 20 sl st to the centre of the first 3 ch space, 3 ch, (1 tr, 3 ch, 2 tr) in the same space, (9 ch, 1 dc in the next 8 ch space) twice, 9 ch, * (2 tr, 3 ch, 2 tr) in the next 3 ch space, (9 ch, 1 dc in the next 8 ch) twice, 9 ch; rep from *, ending with a sl st in the top of the first 3 ch.

Row 21 sl st to the centre of the first 3 ch space, 3 ch, (1 tr, 3 ch, 2 tr) in the same space, 9 ch, miss the next 9 ch space, 1 dc in the next 9 ch space, 9 ch, miss the next 9 ch space, * (2 tr, 3 ch, 2 tr) in the next 3 ch space, 9 ch, miss the next 9 ch space, 1 dc in the next 9 ch space, 9 ch, miss the next 9 ch space; rep from *, ending with a sl st in the top of the first 3 ch.

Row 22 sl st to the centre of the first 3 ch space, 3 ch, (1 tr, 3 ch, 2 tr) in the same space, 9 ch, 1 dc in the next dc, 9 ch, * (2 tr, 3 ch, 2 tr) in the next 3 ch space, 9 ch, 1 dc in the next dc, 9 ch; rep from *, ending with a sl st in the top of the first 3 ch.

Row 23 sl st to the centre of the first 3 ch space, 3 ch, (2 tr, 3 ch, 3 tr) in the same space, 3 ch, 10 dc in the next 9 ch space, 1 dc in the next dc, 10 dc in the next 9 ch space, 3 ch, * (3 tr, 3 ch, 3 tr) in the next 3 ch space, 3 ch, 10 dc in the next 9 ch space, 1 dc in the next dc, 10 dc in the next 9 ch space, 3 ch; rep from *, ending with a sl st in the top of the first 3 ch. Fasten off. Dampen the work, pull into shape, hold with rustless pins until dry.

7

FOUR-POSTER BED

The final chapter is devoted to dressing a four-poster bed. The design is fairly simple overall, but it does require patience to complete it. I have included a blanket in this section. Many people prefer blankets, and this one is a very easy pattern to work. The bedspread, sheet and pillow edgings could also be used alone on a different bed. Having completed the four-poster, you may like to indulge your miniature home even more by reworking the curtains for the window.

BED CURTAINS

Materials

Two 700 metre reels of DMC Broder Machine 30 are enough for the curtains, canopy, bedspread, sheet, and pillow edgings

0.60mm (US #14) crochet hook

Make 89 ch. (The pattern for the curtains, etc. is a multiple of seven plus four ch, plus one turning ch.)

Foundation row 1 dc in second ch from hook, miss 2 ch, 3 tr in next ch, * 3 ch, miss 3 ch, 1 dc in next ch, miss 2 ch, 3 tr in next ch; rep from *, ending with 1 ch, turn.

Pattern row 1 dc in first st, 3 tr in next dc, * 3 ch, 1 dc in 3 ch space, 3 tr in next dc; rep from *, ending with 1 ch, turn.

Rep pattern row for length required, allowing a little extra if using ties. Fasten off.

I have used four curtains at the head of the bed only, but if you wish to make additional curtains for the end of the bed the quantity of thread given will be more than sufficient.

 # CANOPY

Work a length of chain (divisible by 3, plus 3 turning ch) to measure across the top of the bed. 1 tr in fourth ch from hook, 1 tr in each ch to end, 3 ch, turn.

Work in rows of tr for length required, end last row with 1 ch, turn.

Foundation row 1 dc in first st, miss 1 st, 3 tr in next st, * 3 ch, 1 dc in next st, miss 1 st, 3 tr in next st; rep from *, ending with 1 ch, turn.

Pattern row 1 dc in first st, 3 tr in dc, * 3 ch, 1 dc in 3 ch space, 3 tr in dc; rep from *, ending with 1 ch, turn.

Rep pattern row for length required. Fasten off. Rejoin thread to chain edge with a sl st, 1 ch; rep the foundation row. Work as for first side. Fasten off.

Long side pieces

Rejoin thread to first side st with a sl st, 2 ch, work a row of trebles divisible by 3. Work foundation row and pattern row as before.

Sew the side pieces to each other and fit over the canopy. If the posts are higher than the canopy, as in the illustration, then leave a small gap at each corner to fit over the posts. Gather each curtain at the top edge, sew inside the canopy leaving a gap at each corner for the bedposts. Run a gathering line 6.5cm (2½in) from the bottom edge of each curtain and tie to bedposts.

BEDSPREAD

Top

Make a length of chain divisible by 7, plus 4, plus 1 turning chain. This should measure between the bedposts. I worked 110 ch, which gave me 15 complete patterns.

Work foundation row as on curtains, cont in pattern until work measures length required, allowing an overhang at bottom edge of bedspread. Fasten off.

First side piece

Measure against the bed and mark where the bottom bedposts are with a length of coloured thread. ** Rejoin thread to top of bedspread with a sl st, 1 ch, work a row of double crochet as far as the mark, making sure the sts are divisible by 7, plus 4, 1 ch, turn.

Foundation row 1 dc in first st, miss 2 dc, 3 tr in next dc, * 3 ch, miss 3 dc, 1 dc in next dc, miss 2 dc, 3 tr in next dc; rep from *, ending with 1 ch, turn.

Cont in pattern as on curtains for length required, this should measure the same as the overhang at the bottom. Fasten off. **

Second side piece

Working from the marker rather than the top edge, rejoin thread with a sl st. Work from ** to ** as on first side piece. Do not fasten off.

Work another pattern row all around bedspread, including extra overhang and corners at the bottom of the bedspread, and the top edge. Work extra sts at the corners so the cover lies flat.

SHEETS AND PILLOWS

SHEETS

Cut the cotton lawn to the required size, approximately 30.5 x 21.5cm (12 x 8½in), allowing plenty to tuck under the mattress. Hem each sheet by hand or machine.

Edging

Work a length of chain approx, one and a quarter times the width of the top sheet, working a multiple of 7 ch, plus 4, plus 1 turning ch. Work the foundation row as on the bed curtains. Rep the pattern row three times. Sew to top edge of sheet with a sl st, easing in fullness.

PILLOWS

Make two pillows, cut cotton lawn 12.5 x 4.5 cm (5 x 1¾in), fold in half.

Allowing 0.5cm (¼in) seam, and using a tiny backstitch, sew one long seam, the short seam and half the second long seam. Turn pillow right side out, stuff lightly with polyester filling, slipstitch the remaining seam to close.

Edging

Work a length of chain approx. one and a half times the length required, working a multiple of 7 ch, plus 4, plus 1 turning chain. Work the foundation row as on the bed curtains. Rep the pattern row twice. Attach to the pillow using a sl st, adjusting gathers; pay particular attention to the corners to keep them flat.

Materials

Cotton lawn or bought sheets and pillows

Small amount of polyester wadding for pillows.

① BLANKET

Materials

One-ply acrylic yarn (approx. 120 metres)

1.25mm (US #8) crochet hook

Make 82 ch loosely.

Foundation row (1 tr, 1 ch, 1 tr) in fourth ch from hook, * miss next ch, (1 tr, 1 ch, 1 tr) in next ch; rep from * to last 2 ch, miss next ch, 1 tr in last ch, 3 ch, turn.

Pattern row Miss first 2 sts, * (1 tr, 1 ch, 1 tr) in next 1 ch space; rep from * to last ch space, miss next st, 1 tr in turning ch, 3 ch, turn.

Rep the pattern row 48 times, or for length required, working 1 ch at end of last row, turn.

Miss first st, 1 dc in each tr and 1 ch space across row, 1 dc in turning ch, 1 ch, turn.

Work in rows of dc for 2cm (¾in). Fasten off.

This is a brief list of specialist suppliers known to me. It does not claim to be complete, and no disrespect is intended to suppliers not listed here. Internet users will find many others listed on enthusiasts' and manufacturers' websites.

One-ply yarn should be available from most miniaturist stores and fairs, as should miniature buttons, buckles, jewellery findings, etc.

United Kingdom

Tim Parker
124 Corhampton Road
Bournemouth
Dorset BH6 5NZ
Tel: +44 (0)1202 429455
Email: timparker@cyberlink.co.uk
Website: www.cyberlink.co.uk/timparker
(Threads)

Silken Strands
20, Y Rhos
Bangor, Gwynedd
Wales LL57 2LT
Tel: +44 (0)1248 362361
Email: silkenstrands@yahoo.co.uk
Website: www.silkenstrands.co.uk
(Threads)

Dixie Collection
PO Box 575
Bromley
Kent BR2 7WP
Tel: +44 (0) 2084620700
Website: www.dixiecollection.co.uk

Tee Pee Crafts
28 Holborn Drive
Mackworth
Derby DE22 4DX
Tel: +44 (0)1332 332772
Email: info@teepeecrafts.co.uk
Website: www.teepeecrafts.co.uk
(Silk ribbon and jewellery findings)

Jojay Crafts
Moore Road
Bourton-on-the-Water
Gloucestershire GL54 2BU
Tel: +44 (0)1451 810081
Email: sales@jojays.com
Website: www.jojays.co.uk
(Fan sticks, buckles, etc.)

The Dolls' House Draper
PO Box 128, Lightcliffe
Halifax
West Yorkshire HX3 8RN
Tel: +44 (0) 1422 201275
(Silk ribbon, buckles, hair combs, buttons)

United States of America

Needlework in Miniature
1852 28th Avenue
San Francisco, CA 94122
Email: nim@pobox.com
Website: www.angelfire.com/ma2/vmsw/nim
(Crochet hooks, DMC Fil à Dentelles 80)

Lacis
3163 Adeline Street
Berkeley, CA 94703
Tel: 510-843-7188
Email: staff@lacis.com
Website: www.lacis.com
(Crochet hooks, DMC Fil à Dentelles 80)

The Lacemaker
4602 Mahoning Avenue NW, Suite C
Warren, OH 44483
Tel: 330-847-6535/800-747-2220
Email: tracy@lacemakerusa.com
Website: www.lacemakerusa.com
(Cotton and linen threads)

Mainland Embroidery Supplies
PO Box 1106
Friendswood, TX 77549
Tel: 800-879-2970/281-482-4877
Email: sales@mainlandes.com
Website: www.mainlandes.com
(Madeira threads)

Madeira USA Ltd
30 Bayside Ct
PO Box 6068
Laconia, NH 03246
Tel: 603-528-2944
Website: www.madeirausa.com
(Madeira threads)

Lacy Susan (Susan Wenzel)
4569 Rincon Place
Dumfries, VA 22026-1045
Tel: 703-508-1114
Email: lacysusan5@aol.com
Website: www.lacysusan.com
(Madeira threads)

Canada

Swallowhill Miniatures
Joy & John Parker
Box 34, Midland
Ontario L4R 4K6
Website: www.swallowhilldolls.com
(One-ply yarn)

Trillium
Ottawa, Ontario
Tel. 613-234-9791
Email: trillium@magma.ca
Website: www.trilliumlace.ca
(Madeira threads)

Australia

Penguin Threads
Website: www.penguin-threads.com.au
(Madeira threads)

Thumbelina
Margaret Morgan
PO Box 242
Henley Beach
South Australia 5022
Tel: (08) 8356 3437
Email: thumblna@senet.com.au
(Lacemaking supplies, threads, etc.)

Jeannette Fishwick
59 Summerleas Road
Fern Tree
Tasmania
7054
Australia
Website: www.miniknitting.com

Australian Craft Network
Website: www.auscraftnet.com.au

Crochet Australia
Email: vicki@crochetaustralia.com.au
Website: www.crochetaustralia.com.au
(DMC Fil à Dentelles 80, crochet hooks)

ABOUT THE AUTHOR

Roz Walters was born in the north-east of England but has lived most of her life in Yorkshire. She was working as a library assistant at Leeds University in the mid-nineties when she was given a dolls' house for her birthday, and her love of creating in miniature was born. When her ideas began to outgrow her own dolls' house, she began creating items in both crochet and cross stitch for various miniaturist magazines.

Roz is an active member of four different postal miniaturists' clubs in the UK and America. She also maintains her own website, totally designed by herself, at www.rozminiatures.co.uk and can be contacted by email at roz@rozminiatures.co.uk

GMC Publications

BOOKS

DOLLS' HOUSES AND MINIATURES

1/12 Scale Character Figures for the Dolls' House	*James Carrington*
Americana in 1/12 Scale: 50 Authentic Projects	
	Joanne Ogreenc & Mary Lou Santovec
The Authentic Georgian Dolls' House	*Brian Long*
A Beginners' Guide to the Dolls' House Hobby	*Jean Nisbett*
Celtic, Medieval and Tudor Wall Hangings in 1/12 Scale Needlepoint	
	Sandra Whitehead
Creating Decorative Fabrics: Projects in 1/12 Scale	*Janet Storey*
Dolls' House Accessories, Fixtures and Fittings	*Andrea Barham*
Dolls' House Furniture: Easy-to-Make Projects in 1/12 Scale	*Freida Gray*
Dolls' House Makeovers	*Jean Nisbett*
Dolls' House Window Treatments	*Eve Harwood*
Edwardian-Style Hand-Knitted Fashion for 1/12 Scale Dolls	
	Yvonne Wakefield
How to Make Your Dolls' House Special: Fresh Ideas for Decorating	
	Beryl Armstrong
Making 1/12 Scale Wicker Furniture for the Dolls' House	*Sheila Smith*
Making Miniature Chinese Rugs and Carpets	*Carol Phillipson*
Making Miniature Food and Market Stalls	*Angie Scarr*
Making Miniature Gardens	*Freida Gray*
Making Miniature Oriental Rugs & Carpets	*Meik & Ian McNaughton*
Making Miniatures: Projects for the 1/12 Scale Dolls' House	
	Christiane Berridge
Making Period Dolls' House Accessories	*Andrea Barham*
Making Tudor Dolls' Houses	*Derek Rowbottom*
Making Upholstered Furniture in 1/12 Scale	*Janet Storey*
Medieval and Tudor Needlecraft: Knights and Ladies in 1/12 Scale	
	Sandra Whitehead
Miniature Bobbin Lace	*Roz Snowden*
Miniature Crochet: Projects in 1/12 Scale	*Roz Walters*
Miniature Embroidered Patchwork: Projects in 1/12 Scale	
	Margaret Major
Miniature Embroidery for the Georgian Dolls' House	*Pamela Warner*
Miniature Embroidery for the Tudor and Stuart Dolls' House	
	Pamela Warner
Miniature Embroidery for the 20th-Century Dolls' House	*Pamela Warner*
Miniature Embroidery for the Victorian Dolls' House	*Pamela Warner*
Miniature Needlepoint Carpets	*Janet Granger*
The Modern Dolls' House	*Jean Nisbett*
More Miniature Oriental Rugs & Carpets	*Meik & Ian McNaughton*
Needlepoint 1/12 Scale: Design Collections for the Dolls' House	
	Felicity Price
New Ideas for Miniature Bobbin Lace	*Roz Snowden*
Patchwork Quilts for the Dolls' House: 20 Projects in 1/12 Scale	
	Sarah Williams
Simple Country Furniture Projects in 1/12 Scale	*Alison J. White*

CRAFTS

Bargello: A Fresh Approach to Florentine Embroidery	*Brenda Day*
Bead and Sequin Embroidery Stitches	*Stanley Levy*
Beginning Picture Marquetry	*Lawrence Threadgold*
Blackwork: A New Approach	*Brenda Day*
Celtic Backstitch	*Helen Hall*
Celtic Cross Stitch Designs	*Carol Phillipson*
Celtic Knotwork Designs	*Sheila Sturrock*
Celtic Knotwork Handbook	*Sheila Sturrock*
Celtic Spirals and Other Designs	*Sheila Sturrock*
Celtic Spirals Handbook	*Sheila Sturrock*
Complete Pyrography	*Stephen Poole*
Creating Made-to-Measure Knitwear:	
A Revolutionary Approach to Knitwear Design	*Sylvia Wynn*
Creative Backstitch	*Helen Hall*
Creative Log-Cabin Patchwork	*Pauline Brown*
Creative Machine Knitting	*GMC Publications*
Cross-Stitch Designs from China	*Carol Phillipson*
Cross-Stitch Designs from India	*Carol Phillipson*
Cross-Stitch Floral Designs	*Joanne Sanderson*
Cross-Stitch Gardening Projects	*Joanne Sanderson*
Decoration on Fabric: A Sourcebook of Ideas	*Pauline Brown*
Decorative Beaded Purses	*Enid Taylor*
Designing and Making Cards	*Glennis Gilruth*
Designs for Pyrography and Other Crafts	*Norma Gregory*
Dried Flowers: A Complete Guide	*Lindy Bird*
Easy Wedding Planner	*Jenny Hopkin*
Exotic Textiles in Needlepoint	*Stella Knight*
Glass Engraving Pattern Book	*John Everett*
Glass Painting	*Emma Sedman*
Handcrafted Rugs	*Sandra Hardy*
Hand-Dyed Yarn Craft Projects	*Debbie Tomkies*
Hobby Ceramics: Techniques and Projects for Beginners	
	Patricia A. Waller
How to Arrange Flowers: A Japanese Approach to English Design	
	Taeko Marvelly
How to Make First-Class Cards	*Debbie Brown*
An Introduction to Crewel Embroidery	*Mave Glenny*
Machine-Knitted Babywear	*Christine Eames*
Making Fabergé-Style Eggs	*Denise Hopper*
Making Fairies and Fantastical Creatures	*Julie Sharp*
Making Hand-Sewn Boxes: Techniques and Projects	*Jackie Woolsey*
Making Kumihimo: Japanese Interlaced Braids	*Rodrick Owen*
Making Mini Cards, Gift Tags & Invitations	*Glennis Gilruth*
Making Polymer Clay Cards and Tags	*Jacqui Eccleson*
Making Wirecraft Cards	*Kate MacFadyen*
Native American Bead Weaving	*Lynne Garner*
New Ideas for Crochet: Stylish Projects for the Home	*Darsha Capaldi*
Paddington Bear in Cross-Stitch	*Leslie Hills*
Papercraft Projects for Special Occasions	*Sine Chesterman*
Papermaking and Bookbinding: Coastal Inspirations	*Joanne Kaar*
Patchwork for Beginners	*Pauline Brown*
Pyrography Designs	*Norma Gregory*
Rose Windows for Quilters	*Angela Besley*
Silk Painting for Beginners	*Jill Clay*
Sponge Painting	*Ann Rooney*
Stained Glass: Techniques and Projects	*Mary Shanahan*

MAGAZINES

WOODTURNING ❧ WOODCARVING ❧ FURNITURE & CABINETMAKING
THE ROUTER ❧ NEW WOODWORKING ❧ THE DOLLS' HOUSE MAGAZINE
OUTDOOR PHOTOGRAPHY ❧ BLACK & WHITE PHOTOGRAPHY
KNITTING ❧ GUILD NEWS

The above represents a full list of all titles currently published or scheduled to be published.
All are available direct from the Publishers or through bookshops, newsagents and specialist retailers.
To place an order, or to obtain a complete catalogue, contact:

GMC Publications,
Castle Place, 166 High Street, Lewes, East Sussex BN7 1XU, United Kingdom
Tel: 01273 488005 Fax: 01273 402866
E-mail: pubs@thegmcgroup.com Website: www.gmcbooks.com

Orders by credit card are accepted